**Public Aid to Nonpublic
Schools**

Lexington Books Politics of Education Series
Frederick M. Wirt, Editor

Michael W. Kirst, Ed., *State, School, and Politics: Research Directions*

Joel S. Berke, Michael W. Kirst, *Federal Aid to Education: Who Benefits? Who Governs?*

Al J. Smith, Anthony Downs, M. Leanne Lachman, *Achieving Effective Desegregation*

Kern Alexander, K. Forbis Jordan, *Constitutional Reform of School Finance*

George R. LaNoue, Bruce L.R. Smith, *The Politics of School Decentralization*

David J. Kirby, T. Robert Harris, Robert L. Crain, Christine H. Rossell, *Political Strategies in Northern School Desegregation*

Philip K. Piele, John Stuart Hall, *Budgets, Bonds, and Ballots: Voting Behavior in School Financial Elections*

John C. Hogan, *The Schools, the Courts, and the Public Interest*

Jerome T. Murphy, *State Education Agencies and Discretionary Funds*

Howard Hamilton, Sylvan Cohen, *Policy-making by Plebiscite*

Daniel J. Sullivan, *Public Aid to Nonpublic Schools*

Public Aid to Nonpublic Schools

Daniel J. Sullivan
Middlebury College

Lexington Books
D. C. Heath and Company
Lexington, Massachusetts
Toronto   London

Library of Congress Cataloging in Publication Data

Sullivan, Daniel Joseph.
  Public aid to nonpublic schools.

  Bibliography: p.
  1. Private schools—United States—Finance. 2. Federal aid to
education—United States. 3. State aid to education—United States.
I. Title.
LB2825.S735   379'.32'0973   74-14531
ISBN 0-669-96198-1

Published simultaneously in Canada.

Printed in the United States of America.

International Standard Book Number: 0-669-96198-1

Library of Congress Catalog Card Number: 74-14531

To Jeanie:
with much love and
many thanks

Contents

viii

List of Figures

ix

List of Tables

Preface

Over the last several years, dissatisfaction with this nation's elementary and secondary schools seems to have increased markedly. Several best-selling books have been published on the subject of why the schools have "failed." Several advisory commissions and task forces—among them a President's Commission on School Finance and a President's Panel on Nonpublic Education—have been established by various governments to find new solutions to the schools' problems. Increasingly, many people have come to believe that the schools' difficulties begin with the way in which they are financed, with the result that questions of school finance have become an important social issue.

Discussions of appropriate policies for financing our elementary and secondary schools have focused on three issues. The first, an outgrowth of the so-called Taxpayers Revolt, is whether traditional sources of revenue, particularly the local property tax, are still adequate for funding ever-increasing education expenditures. The second issue, stimulated by a series of recent court decisions, concerns finding more equitable ways of financing schools, ways which will not make the quality of a child's schooling a function of wealth. Finally, as enrollments have fallen sharply in the nonpublic schools, there has been increasing concern over the financial status of these schools and what assistance the public sector might provide. To date, the first two issues have received the lion's share of attention, especially from economists doing policy analysis. The third issue has been almost neglected by analysts, with the result that the public debate has remained at a very elementary level. In part, this situation has been a consequence of the first two issues seeming more central to the general debate and their affecting larger numbers of people. However, as policymakers look more and more to institutional restructuring as the key to improving our schools, the appropriate policy toward nonpublic schools becomes more and more important.

This study is an effort to add to the current public debate on the nonpublic schools. It is done in the belief that economics is a most useful framework for considering questions of public aid to these schools. Because the debate has focused almost exclusively on existing nonpublic schools, and because the new legislation being proposed is aimed at this constituency, I believed that it was most useful to limit the analysis to appropriate policies toward these schools. It is hoped, however, that the theoretical analysis presented here provides some insights into what might happen if a policy designed to radically alter the nonpublic sector, such as a universal voucher, were enacted.

As an introduction to the analysis, this book begins with a discussion of the extent of the current debate on aid to nonpublic schools and a discussion of the general context of that debate—the growing general dissatisfaction with our nation's schools. Chapter 2 provides further background, examining current enrollment and finance patterns in the nonpublic schools and trying to empirically determine what factors are affecting equilibrium enrollments in these schools. Chapters 3, 4, and 5 form the heart of the analysis. Chapter 3 makes use of public goods theory to develop a model for determining an optimal role of government in education for a variety of assumptions about market conditions and constraints on the various participants. Chapter 4 then analyzes the traditional arguments for and against public aid to nonpublic schools, both in light of Chapter 3 and in light of the empirical evidence available; it tries to show that the case for aiding these schools is at best tenuous. Finally, Chapter 5 considers what public policies toward the existing nonpublic schools are appropriate. It finds that the policies currently being espoused to "save" these schools are the least justifiable on theoretical grounds and amount to poor public policy.

This study was begun while I was at the Brookings Institution. It was part of a research project conducted jointly with Robert Reischauer and Robert Hartman, which resulted in the book *Reforming School Finance*. Much of the research presented here formed the basis for Chapter 5 of that book. Both of the other authors provided valuable assistance to my work. In the early stages, Robert Reischauer provided a number of helpful ideas and suggestions. Robert Hartman wrote many valuable comments on various drafts of this manuscript. I wish to thank them both for their contributions. I also wish to thank the Edna McConnell Clark Foundation, which funded the school finance project, and the Brookings Institution, which gave me considerable time to continue this work after the project was finished and which has given me permission to use here many of the tables from chapters 2, 5, and 6 of *Reforming School Finance* (© 1973 by the Brookings Institution, Washington, D. C.). In addition, I am thankful for the valuable secretarial assistance provided by Virginia Crum and Margaret Su of Brookings and Teri Wistrom of the University of Minnesota's School of Public Affairs, as well as for the production of the final manuscript done by Karen Daninger.

I would also like to thank Richard Nelson, Stephen Dresch, and David Stern for their helpful comments and suggestions—particularly Richard Nelson. Beginning with my first inquiries into the subject and continuing through various formulations of the problem, Nelson has continually provided useful comments and criticisms that have helped to greatly improve the final product.

Finally and most importantly, I would like to thank my wife, Jeanie. Her helpful comments have made this study much more coherent than it otherwise would have been; and without her support and encouragement, it would likely never have been completed.

Public Aid to Nonpublic Schools

1

Introduction

The nonpublic elementary and secondary schools in the United States have long been an integral part of the nation's educational establishment –supplementing in an important way the main task of our public school system. . . . This government cannot be indifferent to the potential collapse of such schools.

Richard Nixon (Message to
Congress, March 1970)

In recent years the alleged financial plight of the nation's nonpublic elementary and secondary schools has become a matter of increasing public concern. Cost in these schools are rising at a much more rapid rate than in their public counterparts; and as enrollments continue to decline at high rates, many people are concerned whether the nonpublic schools will be able to continue as a viable alternative to the public system. A number of people are clamouring for large government subsidies to bail out the existing nonpublic schools.

Consideration of giving public aid to nonpublic schools raises a number of economic and social issues, dealing not only with the efficient allocation and the equitable distribution of our nation's potential educational resources, but also with the very structure of our educational system. To date, although there is a growing amount of literature on the subject, the public debate has remained at a very elementary level. There has been little economic analysis of the question; and the research already done, with little exception, has been done in a narrow framework, treating the question as an isolated policy issue.

This study is an effort to add to the current public debate on aid to nonpublic schools. It hopes to do so in three ways: (1) provide a theoretical framework for determining whether any, or which kinds of, public subsidies for nonpublic schools are desirable; (2) in light of this framework analyze the traditional arguments for and against such aid, and analyze the major proposals for aid; and (3) determine whether aid would actually benefit all or some of the existing nonpublic schools. In many instances, because of a lack of data, the empirical analysis is limited to the Roman Catholic schools—which comprise over three-fourths of the existing nonpublic sector. While most of the current debate centers on existing schools,

1

it is hoped that the theoretical analysis presented here will provide some insights into what might happen if a policy designed to radically alter the sector, such as a universal voucher, were enacted. Moreover, where possible, the implications of the Catholic analysis for the rest of the nonpublic sector are set forth.

The remainder of this chapter is an attempt to provide a background for this analysis. I look at the current public debate on aid to nonpublic schools and examine its relation to the more general debate on the state of our nation's schools.

The Current Debate

The public debate on aid to nonpublic schools has expanded rapidly in recent years. The Nixon administration has given the question considerable attention. In addition to his message to Congress, the president has delivered two major addresses on the subject, to the Knights of Columbus in New York in August 1971 and to the National Catholic Education Association in Philadelphia in April 1972, emphasizing the point that, "I am irrevocably committed to these propositions: America needs her nonpublic schools. Those nonpublic schools need help. Therefore, we must and will find ways to provide that help."[1] He reemphasized this position during his 1972 reelection campaign[2] and submitted specific aid proposals as part of his State of the Union message, delivered to Congress in February 1973.

In March 1970, the president established the President's Commission on School Finance, which was to study and report to the president on all aspects of financing elementary and secondary education. The mandate the president gave the commission prominently mentioned nonpublic schools; of the seventeen tasks he outlined for it, seven dealt specifically, in whole or in part, with nonpublic schools.[3] Moreover, a month later, the president established a separate President's Panel on Nonpublic Education, which was essentially a subcommittee of the full commission.[4] Both of these groups issued their final reports in 1972, making a number of recommendations as to what the government should do for nonpublic schools (for discussion, see Appendix 1A).

The Democrats have also taken an interest in the nonpublic school issue. All of the Democratic presidential candidates frequently endorsed such aid during the 1972 campaign. Over 200 bills were introduced in the 92nd Congress to provide general assistance to nonpublic schools.[5] Moreover, several days of public hearings were held by the powerful House Ways and Means Committee on aid in the form of tax credits, and the committee actually reported out a bill which may get favorable consideration in the 93rd Congress.[6]

There is similar widespread interest at the state level. Over one-fourth of the states from all parts of the country have established special commissions to study the question of aid to nonpublic schools and to make recommendations to the state legislatures.[a] Moreover, twenty states passed new laws providing for aid to nonpublic schools in the last two years, and a third of the states have new aid programs pending before their legislatures.[7]

Although the large majority of prominent politicians appear to be in favor of aid to nonpublic schools, there are many groups in the nation who oppose such aid. The National Education Association has strongly opposed aid to nonpublic schools, arguing that scarce public revenues should be used to meet the unmet needs of the public schools.[8] Similarly, the AFL-CIO has voiced opposition to the aid programs now before Congress.[9] A number of groups, including the American Civil Liberties Union, PEARL (People for Educational and Religious Liberty), and POAU (Protestants and Other Americans United), have opposed aid on constitutional grounds.[10] Some religious denominations, among them the Baptists and Unitarians, and church leaders have opposed aid on the grounds that it would bring government interference in religion and destroy the distinctive nature of sectarian schools.

In fact, although never mentioned publicly by the politicians, much of their consensus in favor of aid appears to be based on a desire of politicians to gain the support of one segment of the electorate: the Roman Catholics.[11] Some political analysts believe that the "Catholic vote" is up for grabs. While traditionally the Catholics have voted Democratic, because of their economic status and the party's domestic policy, more recently they have become attuned to the Republican party's philosophy, particularly on foreign policy.[12] In a number of key political states, Catholics represent a sizable fraction of the population and hence any shift in their voting patterns could be significant (see Table 1-1). Some persons believe that opposition to aid by the National Education Association and the American Federation of Teachers is also largely political—these groups desire to achieve as strong a position as possible in American education, and expansion of the nonpublic sector would dilute their influence.[b]

General public opinion seems to be fairly well divided on the issue. A recent Gallup poll found that 48 percent of the country favored "giving some government tax money to help parochial schools," while 44 percent opposed the idea.[13] Even parents of public school students (47 percent

---

[a]These states include: Colorado, Illinois, Maryland, Michigan, Minnesota, New Hampshire, New York, South Dakota, Washington, Wisconsin, Rhode Island, Massachusetts, and California.

[b]While these two groups represent teachers in over two-thirds of the nation's public school systems, they represent teachers in only one out of twenty Catholic school systems.

Table 1-1

Catholics as a Percentage of Population in 1972 for the States with the Eight Largest Number of Presidential Electoral Votes

State	Catholics as Percentage of Total Population
California	21
New York	35
Pennsylvania	31
Illinois	32
Texas	18
Ohio	21
Michigan	26
New Jersey	42
U.S. Average	23

Sources: U.S. Bureau of the Census, *Statistical Abstract of the United States, 1972* (1972) p. 13; and *Official Catholic Directory, 1972*, insert following pt. 4.

favor, 47 percent opposed) and adults with no children in school (47 percent favor, 44 percent opposed) were evenly divided.[19] This division represents a slightly more favorable posture towards aid then the public held four years earlier—a 1966 Gallup survey found that only 38 percent favored aid while 50 percent opposed.[15] Local and regional surveys conducted during 1970 and 1971 in various parts of the country found similar splits.[16] More recently, in November 1972 three states—Idaho, Maryland and Oregon—had on the ballot referenda dealing with aid to nonpublic schools. All three were defeated by narrow margins. The consensus among political leaders certainly does not hold for the general electorate.[17]

Nature of the Dissatisfaction

The division and the debate over aid to nonpublic schools are in fact very much a part of the much larger debate going on over our nation's public schools. To understand, or at least to analyze, the nonpublic school issue, one must understand the nature of the dissatisfaction being voiced about both the public and nonpublic schools and the types of solutions that are being proposed. The President's Commission on School Finance begins its final report with the assertion that, "For millions of children, American education—both public and nonpublic—is not working as it was intended to work.[18] According to a recent Gallup survey, over a quarter of the parents of our nation's 50 million students agreed with this assertion as it applied to their own children.[19] In addition to the federal commission, a large number of the states have established special commissions within the past few years to study problems of the schools. Their reports contain introductóry remarks similar to the President's Commission.[20] Moreover, the ever growing number of best-selling books on school reform begin with the assertion that the schools have failed.[21]

Implicit in these statements, and the general debate, is the assumption that we know what the schools should be accomplishing or what we want them to accomplish. Historically, the notion of universal schooling and the public school movement grew rapidly in the mid- and late-nineteenth century.[22] The principal argument used to gain support for the movement was a citizenship one: if we were to remain a free people and to keep a republican form of government, then we had to have an educated electorate.[23]

Imbedded in this argument was a goal for the schools of instilling in all youths a common set of values and ideals. As the public-school movement grew, its leaders began to articulate an additional goal: in providing training for future employment, they saw the schools as freeing individuals from the economic status into which they were born and providing for greatly increased economic mobility. The public school movement's position is best summed up by its foremost spokesman, Horace Mann of Massachusetts. On the economic value of education, he wrote:

Education, then, beyond all other devices of human origin, is the great equalizer of the condition of men—the balance wheel of the social machinery. . . . I mean that it gives each man the independence and the means, by which he can resist the selfishness of other men. It does better than to disarm the poor of their hostility towards the rich; it prevents being poor.[24]

Over the years the most often stated goals of education have changed very little. Educators today talk about developing good citizens, preparing people for jobs, and achieving "equal opportunity." Indeed, how well these goals have been accepted by the general society is indicated by a recent Gallup survey of parents which asked why they wanted a good education for their children. The survey found the following results:[25]

1. To get better jobs	44%
2. To get along better with people at all levels of society	43%
3. To make more money—achieve financial success	38%
4. To attain self-satisfaction	21%
5. To stimulate their minds	15%
6. Miscellaneous reasons	11%

Orthodox economists have been similarly consistent in their views on education, views which parallel the conventional wisdom. Beginning with Adam Smith, they saw the role of education in producing good citizens. The classical economists, with their utilitarian background, focused on the negative aspects of this goal: they believed that educated or skilled people were less likely to commit crimes against society; hence there were economic returns to education.[26] More recently, economists have focused on the positive benefits of an educated electorate. Milton Friedman, for example, asserts that

A stable and democratic society is impossible without a minimum degree of literacy on the part of most citizens and without widespread acceptance of some common set of values. Education can contribute to both.[27]

Burton Weisbrod makes a similar point:

Without widespread literacy the significance of books, newspapers, and similar media for the transmission of knowledge would dwindle; and it seems fair to say that the communication of information is of vital importance to the maintenance of competition and, indeed, to the existence of a market economy, as well as the maintenance of political democracy. The American voting process would be seriously impaired by widespread illiteracy.[28]

About the middle of the nineteenth century, economists such as J. R. McCulloch began to recognize the role of education in economic growth.[29] This line of thought was extended to the microlevel—people began to note the positive relation between education and income—and led to the concept of schooling as "*human* capital formation," about which there is a substantial literature today.[30] Finally, as economists have turned their attention from simply efficiency considerations to also taking into account the equity aspects of policy issues, they have seen equality of opportunity as a valid goal of education: schools may produce social benefits in the form of income redistribution.[31]

One factor that has changed over the last century is the appropriate relationship between religion and the schools. The first schools in this country had been sectarian ones. However, the principle of separation of church and state was seen as applicable to education; and as early as 1818, states wrote provisions into their constitutions prohibiting public monies from being spent for sectarian instruction.[32] However, what resulted from such prohibitions was not a system of "secular" education, but rather a "nonsectarian" one—that is, religious principles common to all religions were seen as an appropriate part of the "common set of values" mentioned earlier. What this meant in practice was instruction in general Protestant beliefs. The limits of this effort to keep religion in the schools became evident in the latter part of the nineteenth century when millions of Catholics began to immigrate to the United States. What for Protestants was "nonsectarian" was clearly "sectarian" to Catholics. The result of what at times was a bitter struggle was a general agreement that religious instruction must be taken out of the common schools and consigned to the family and the church,[33] and hence the moral instruction took on the appearance of secular humanism.

How closely the principle of complete separation was followed varied widely across the states. Throughout much of the twentieth century, the beliefs of particular sects were taught. It was not until 1963 that the U.S. Supreme Court actually outlawed the recitation of prayers and reading the Bible in public schools,[34] and not until 1968 that it found unconstitutional an Arkansas law prohibiting the teaching of evolution.[35] Even today there are many who believe that we need to find new ways around the "wall of separation." As President Nixon has said:

As we consider the nonpublic schools—whether they are Catholic, Protestant, Jewish, or even nonsectarian—they often add the dimensions of spiritual values in the education process. Children who attend these schools are offered a moral code by which to live. At a time when the trend in education is too often toward impersonal materialism, I believe America needs more, rather than less, emphasis on education which emphasizes moral, religious and spiritual values.[36]

In general it would seem that the goals for the schools of instilling common values, preparing students for jobs, and enhancing socioeconomic mobility are generally agreed upon, even among the schools' critics. The more conservative of these critics would take issue with the relative weight attached to the three goals.[37] More radical critics agree that the first and second are indeed goals of the schools, but point out that the "common values" are actually those of a particular class and that preparing students for jobs does not mean teaching them cognitive skills, but rather specific behavioral patterns.[38] In fact, some recent critics have offered a similar interpretation of the early public school movement. They argue that it was a consequence of the United States developing an industrialized, capitalist economy. As the nature of work changed dramatically and the role of the family diminished, the schools were seen as the ideal institution for inculcating the necessary social values to accept a capitalist economic system and to legitimize its hierarchical division of labor.[39] Finally, while radical critics agree that equal opportunity is a desirable output of the schools, they argue that the reproduction of the social division of labor makes substantial increases in socioeconomic mobility impossible.[40] Recently another group has argued that schools do nothing substantive in behalf of the second and third goals. These critics view education as a screening device—that is, education merely bestows credentials that improve a person's position in the labor market without raising his or her productivity (see Lester C. Thurow, "Education and Economic Equality," and Paul Taubman and Terence Wales, "Education as an Investment and a Screening Device").

Both groups of critics focus their criticism on the schools' failure to achieve stated goals. There are two main thrusts to that criticism. The first concerns preparing students for future employment. Some critics believe that the schools do a very poor job of this, principally because the schools are too regimented, too concerned with discipline and order, and hence stifle or destroy students' creativity.[41] Critics such as Jonathan Kozol and George Dennison make the point even more strongly, arguing that the background and lives of the pupils must be taken into account, that it is the way school affects the lives of students and their self-concept that is important, that cognitive development cannot take place apart from emotional development, and that neither can take place in a rigid, militaristic environment that continually represses student initiative—the sort of environment particularly found in schools serving the urban poor, but also in more subtle ways in middle-class schools.[42] The more radical critics criticize the schools on this point for a very different reason: they see the schools as being all too successful in socializing students to accept the totalitarian and alienating hierarchical division of labor.[43] That is, they argue persuasively that the thrust of the above criticism is misguided; schools are doing exactly what capitalists want and if we are to change this aspect of social relations in the schools, we must change the social relations of work.

Orthodox economists have joined in the criticism, focusing for the most part on the minor role that schools seem to play in a student's academic achievement.[44] They attribute this fact in part to our lack of a good model or theory of learning.[45] But even more, many have noted that the incentives to do a good job are very weak, largely because teachers and administrators are not very accountable to the consuming public, and because their personal reward structures are not very closely related to student success. As a result, this has led many to feel that schools are wasting resources and not operating in a cost efficient manner.[46] The result of rapidly rising costs with little perceived change in output has been a so-called Taxpayers Revolt. School bond issues have been voted down in ever-increasing numbers,[47] and considerable additional pressure for school reform has arisen.[48]

The second major thrust of the criticism focuses on the school's apparent failure to achieve their goal of equal opportunity. In part that debate has focused on just what one means by "equal opportunity."[49] But a large amount of the criticism is much stronger. Silberman, for example, argues that

far from being 'the great equalizer,' the schools help perpetuate the differences in condition. . . . The failure is not new; it is one the United States has tolerated for a century or more. The public school never has done much of a job of educating youngsters from the lower class or from immigrant homes.[50]

He goes on to discuss how in recent years the public schools have particularly failed in educating minority groups in large urban centers, "less because of maliciousness than because of mindlessness.[51] He places great emphasis on two factors: the seeming desire of educators to force children to fit the school rather than adapting the school to the particular students it services and the self-fulfilling expectation of many inner-city teachers that their students *cannot* learn.[52]

Other critics, particularly those who have themselves taught in inner-city schools, see this failure as closely linked to the first: the focus on discipline, particularly in urban minority schools, makes these places dismal and unsuited to learning. In large part they believe this situation is brought about by the choice of cognitive achievement, as measured by standardized test scores, as the principal measure of output. They cite the cultural biases in such tests and students' varying ability to perform in test situations; and they argue that as a result schools focus on outputs least relevant to the lives of poor youths, hence creating an alienating situation.[53] Again the radical critics point out that inequality of outcomes is necessary in a capitalist economy and that reform implies changing the social relations of work.[54]

More recently, many people have come to argue that the schools' failure to achieve their goal of equal opportunity really begins with the way in which schools are financed, that is, the manner in which educational services are rationed.[55] They assert that reliance on the local property tax as the principal source of revenue for the nation's schools means that less funds are available to be spent on schools serving the poor than schools serving children of wealthy families, because families with low incomes live in areas with low property-tax values.[56] This criticism has taken the form of legal challenges to existing finance systems in various states. The lower courts have ruled favorably on several of these suits in at least seven different states.[57] Recently the U.S. Supreme Court overturned one of these decisions.[58] However, the California and New Jersey cases were decided on the basis of their respective state constitutions and hence still stand. Moreover, the 5-4 division in the Supreme Court suggests that in the future this decision may be reversed. In any event, the mere litigation of the various cases has provided a substantial new impetus to school finance reform.

As with many public-service problems, education critics have proposed three types of remedies for the schools' failures: (1) allocate more resources to education; (2) reallocate existing resources (i.e., change technologies); or (3) reorganize resources (i.e., change institutional structures).[59] Early critics concerned with the goal of equal opportunity focused on the first type of solution. They noted the serious inequalities in resources resulting from use of the local property tax mentioned above. Moreover, they argued that if large additional sums were spent in schools serving the poor, their educational handicaps could be overcome. This approach, commonly referred to as "compensatory education," has had far less success than was anticipated, although the evidence is far from clear.[60]

Throughout the latter part of the 1960s, critics concerned with the schools' failure to educate began to focus on the second type of reform. New "technologies" such as team teaching, programmed instruction, the open classroom and computer-assisted instruction were heralded as the way of the future. For most of these, the results of numerous experiments have yet to produce conclusive results.[61] Economists attempting to aid education in their search for solutions to the schools' problems have concentrated largely on developing an "education production function."[62] Hopefully, such a production function would indicate which types of resources should be expanded and which types contracted—and presumably could lead to what Benson refers to as "technological efficiency."[63] However, the wide variety of studies done have mostly served to point up how limited our knowledge is: available measures of output are seriously inadequate, and our knowledge of what inputs really are, let alone in what way they impact on outputs, is minimal. There has been one consistent and clear result: no single variant of schooling tried to date dominates all others. We seem to be in a "flat region" where minor changes in school technology have little impact.[64]

More recently, education policymakers and economists alike have begun to focus their attention on the third type of solution, arguing that the schools as they are now are resistant to change, or that there are no incentives for them to change.[65] Many believe that only these kinds of solutions can produce changes substantial enough to have a real effect on school outcomes. Proposals have ranged from simply decentralizing large systems such as is being done in New York City to the complete privatization of the schools by means of a voucher system.[66] The hope is that by changing the governance of schools, we may be able to alter the social relations of the schools and hence substantially alter outcomes.[67] In the form that the arguments for such changes are made, their object is to directly affect the goals of *how* school outputs should be produced (see below). It is argued that schools will operate with greater efficiency, that they will be more inclined to produce the set of outputs desired by consumers, and that there will be greater diversity and competition among schools.[68] Moreover, many economists have joined these critics, arguing that the more a free market is introduced into education, the more accountable the schools will be and the stronger the incentives will be to adopt the best educational technologies.[69] Implicit is the belief that such changes will increase the desired outputs.[c]

---

[c]The one goal that many feel the market is least likely to produce is equal opportunity. In fact, most of the complications of various proposed institutional reforms are the result of an effort to protect this objective.

Implicit in this debate over our nation's schools and in the types of solutions offered is the basic paradigm, or perspective, most often used to view our schools. That paradigm is an economic one: we talk of the education "industry," and schools are seen as "producing" education and students "consuming" it. This approach has led us to have an additional set of goals about *how* the schools are to function.

Schools should be *efficient;* they should produce a certain quality product at lowest possible cost. *Pluralism* becomes a goal; diversity and competition are viewed as assets.[d] Moreover, treating the output of schools as "products" creates the need to be able to measure that output, to be able to quantify the goals of education. Finally, any consideration of the appropriate government role in education is done in terms of "how would the private market fail to accomplish these tasks."

Users of this paradigm are not limited to academic economists doing research in education. Other types of researchers such as psychologists and sociologists place a similar emphasis on output and the ability to measure that output. The principle exceptions are the so-called reform writers who seek to focus on students' lives.[70] But more importantly, the economic paradigm or functional equivalent appears to be the principal approach of persons in policy positions in government. Hence its impact on government legislation is a very real one.

The nonpublic schools educate only a small part of our nation's elementary and secondary students. The present system of schooling in this country is dominated by a system of "pure communal provision" at the local level;[71] there are roughly 17,000 publicly controlled and operated school districts in this country which educate approximately 90 percent of all elementary and secondary students. These districts are run by local governments. While state and federal governments place some constraints on the actions of local school district officials, their principal role in our school system is in affecting the allocation of resources to, and within, education through various subsidy programs.

The debate over existing nonpublic schools is in part related to the question of whether we can improve education technology—in providing competition and diversity, are existing nonpublic schools a source of education innovation? Even more, however, the nonpublic schools' debate is an integral part of the debate on suggested institutional reforms. Any policy designed to substantially change institutional forms will have an impact on these schools; and any substantial program of aid to nonpublic schools will ultimately have a real impact on the institutional form of

---

[d]A corollary to the goal of pluralism is "accessibility." For nonpublic schools to offer a real alternative, they must be truly accessible. This implies the need to look at limitations to such access which may arise from religious or academic requirements or from economic barriers or distant location.

schooling. Hence, any analysis of aid to nonpublic schools must be done in the context of what institutional form, or set of forms, are most appropriate for the schools, what forms will generate the incentives necessary for the schools to produce a desirable set of outputs. This study will attempt to provide at least part of the answer to this question. It will do so from the point of view of "what is the optimal government involvement in the financing and provision of schooling," and more specifically, within the framework of answering whether or not it should provide assistance to the nonpublic schools. I hope to show that (1) while there may be theoretically justifiable grounds for public subsidies to the nonpublic schools, they are not likely to exist in practice, and most existing nonpublic schools do not qualify for such aid, particularly in light of the substantial aid they already receive; moreover (2) even if they were to receive such aid, it would have little impact on the fiscal crises of most of these schools; and hence (3) the types of aid being proposed to "save" the nonpublic schools are the least justifiable on theoretical grounds.

Chapter 2 provides additional background, examining the present institutional structure of our nation's schools and the role of nonpublic schools in the overall system. Chapters 3 through 5 form the heart of the analysis. Chapter 3 attempts to determine the "optimal" role of government in education for a variety of assumptions about market condition and constraints on the various participants. Chapter 4 then analyzes the traditional arguments for and against aid to nonpublic schools, both in light of Chapter 3 and in light of the empirical evidence available. Chapter 5 then considers what appropriate public policy ought to be, both for the existing institutional structure and for possible alternatives.

One major constraint on possible government policies arises because most existing nonpublic schools are religiously affiliated, and hence the issue of separation of church and state is involved. In a recent ruling, the Supreme Court placed severe limitations on the forms of aid permissible.[72] In later chapters, I analyze a number of programs which would seem to fall outside this ruling. I do so because many of them are still being debated in various legislatures—for some there is always the hope that a future Supreme Court will reverse this decision or that the schools will alter the nature of their religious affiliation to circumvent the decision.[e] But more importantly, I do so to show that even if this constraint is relaxed or circumvented, the policies being currently espoused are undesirable.

---

[e]In considering the legal, as well as economic, characteristics of various policies, I hope to show what types of programs are most likely to get future judicial approval.

Appendix 1A:
Reports of the President's Commission on School Finance and President's Panel on Nonpublic Education

The appropriate governmental role in financing our nation's schools was at least ostensibly the issue with which the recent President's Commission on School Finance dealt. As noted earlier, the Presidental Commission contracted several studies on aid to nonpublic schools. However, its final report dealt only briefly with these schools. The commission expressed the belief that "the public purpose is served by the operation of the nonpublic schools":[1] they provide "diversity, choice and healthy competition to traditional public education"; they "provide a substantial part of the investment in urban education"; and in many inner-city areas they help "preserve at least a semblance of racial balance in these old neighborhoods" by keeping white Catholic families in areas into which racial minorities are moving.[2] After noting that several states and localities would be hard pressed to provide the additional education resources were the nonpublic schools to close, the commission recommended that, where legally permissible, public funds be used to provide a variety of "child benefit" type services. Moreover, believing that more substantial funds would be necessary, the commission recommended that the government study "more substantive forms of assistance."[3]

More detailed analysis of this issue was left to the President's Panel on Nonpublic Education, consisting of four members of the President's Commission, which issued its final report about a month later. The report, which itself is fairly brief, begins with the statement of a three-fold mandate.[4] However, the panel seemingly chose to ignore the first two points; its report includes almost no analysis of the nature of the alleged "crisis" in nonpublic education, or of the rationale for public assistance.[5] Instead, as a prelude to making its recommendations for increased government aid, the panel discusses three points: (1) it believes the nonpublic schools are a national asset for several reasons and asserts that this belief is based on extensive research—although none is presented; (2) it believes that if all nonpublic schools close, there would be a substantial financial burden placed on certain areas and localities—almost no evidence is offered to support this claim; and (3) it discusses extensively why it believes various forms of aid can be found to be constitutional.[6] The panel, asserting that "since the public interest is deeply affected by the fate of nonpublic schools, it follows that the Government may not remain indifferent,"[7] then

13

proceeded to outline a comprehensive program of federal aid, which included the following:

1. *Federal assistance to the urban poor through:* (a) supplemental income allowances for nonpublic school tuitions for welfare recipients and the working poor; (b) experiments with vouchers; (c) full enforcement of ESEA provisions entitling nonpublic school pupils to certain benefits; and (d) an urban assistance program for public and nonpublic schools.

2. *Federal income tax credits for part of nonpublic school tuition.*

3. *Federal construction loan program analogous to the F.H.A. instrumentality for home buyers.*

4. *Tuition reimbursements to insure equity for nonpublic school children in anticipated long-range programs of Federal aid to education.* [8]

In its recommendations, the panel ignored altogether the finding of the full President's Commission that for Roman Catholic schools, which account for virtually all of the crisis, "their survival does not depend totally or even mainly on the amount of money available to them." [9]

The Current Nonpublic System

Like other significant voluntary enterprises in America, nonpublic schools came into being to fill an important need not met by a public agency. They operate under the constant and pervasive challenge of the market: if they fail to measure up to client expectations or if a public agency better serves the purpose, they cease to exist.

> President's Panel on Non-
> public Education (*Final Report*)

As the issue of public aid to the nonpublic schools has been operationalized in the current public debate, there are actually two dimensions to the policies being espoused: (1) public aid to keep the nation's nonpublic schools fiscally solvent and operating; and (2) public aid to maintain enrollments in the existing nonpublic schools. Some persons concerned with the former dimension are interested in preserving choice in schooling, even if that choice is not exercised; others believe it is also important to preserve the autonomy of individual schools (see below). Persons concerned with the second dimension are worried about the possible impact enrollment declines will have on neighboring public schools.[a] While there is some overlap—school closings can cause enrollment declines and vice versa —different types of aid may have relatively different impacts on the two dimensions (see Chapter 5).

To provide a perspective on the dimensions of the aid issue and of the concern implicit in the policies being espoused, this chapter attempts to examine the factors underlying the causes for concern, specifically to look at the factors underlying the supply and demand for existing nonpublic elementary and secondary schools. While they are in many aspects identical and hence often treated as one in the analysis, it should be kept in mind that there is not a single market for nonpublic schooling, but rather a large number of geographically, more-or-less distinct markets. Moreover, it may also be useful to distinguish between two types of nonpublic schools: the sectarian schools, which in many ways are quasi-public, and the unaffiliated or "private" schools. While the economic factors affecting both types are similar in many respects, there are real differences—which this chapter seeks to point out.

---

[a]For a more detailed discussion of these distinctions, see Chapter 4.

Because the available data is somewhat limited and because the same factor may affect both demand and supply, distinguishing between the two sides is not always completely possible. In trying to separate out the independent effects of demand and supply on equilibrium enrollment, the basic approach used has been to estimate the amount of enrollment reduction which can be attributed to a decrease in supply, and then to attribute the remaining reduction to a decline in demand and examine what factors might have caused such a shift. Prior to this analysis, a description of the existing system and the trends in enrollment are presented.

The Current Nonpublic Schools: Enrollments and Finances

In looking at the aggregate picture of enrollments in the nonpublic sector, two points stand out. First, although 5 million students are enrolled in nonpublic elementary and secondary schools, they do not represent a very large part of all elementary and secondary enrollments, currently accounting for only about 10 percent of the total. The second point is that although many people, especially the President's Panel on Nonpublic Education,[1] have emphasized the variety and diversity in the nonpublic schools, the enrollment data is dominated by the Roman Catholic schools, whose students accounted for about four-fifths of the nonpublic total in 1970.[b](see Table 2-1) While a number of other religious organizations operate schools—among them Lutheran, Episcopal, Jewish, and Seventh-Day Adventists—none accounts for more than 4 percent of nonpublic enrollment (0.4 percent of total elementary and secondary enrollment). The diverse set of nonsectarian schools accounts for only 7 percent of the nonpublic total. Hence the notion that "aid to private schools is aid to religious, especially Catholic, schools" is not far from the truth.

These aggregate numbers, however, may be misleading in that they hide the relative importance of nonpublic schools in certain areas and localities. Generally, the pattern of nonpublic enrollment differs greatly from that of public school enrollment. In six states, more than one child in six attends a nonpublic school; in six others, less than one in twenty-five does so (Table 2-2). In terms of absolute numbers, nonpublic enrollments are concentrated in eight states, and even more so in the large cities in these states. The eight states, which have less than 45 percent of total public school enrollment, have over 61 percent of nonpublic enrollment—the eleven cities themselves account for about 20 percent of the national nonpublic total (Tables 2-1 and 2-3).

[b]1970-71 is the last year for which a detailed breakdown is available. In 1973-74, total nonpublic enrollment was 4,945,000. This total may be broken down as follows: Catholic schools — 3,614,000; Lutheran schools — 164,809; NAIS schools — 259,590; and other nonpublic — 906,601.

Table 2-1

Distribution of Enrollment in Nonpublic Schools, by Church Relationship, 1970-71 School Year

Church Relation and Denomination	Enrollment	Percentage of Total Non-public School Enrollment	Percentage of Total Public and Non-public School Enrollment
Total	5,282,567	100.0	10.4
Church Related	4,911,731	93.0	9.7
Catholic	4,367,323	82.7	8.6
Lutheran	206,020	3.9	0.4
Seventh Day Adventist	52,826	1.0	0.1
Jewish	68,673	1.3	0.1
Episcopal	53,040	1.0	0.1
Christian (National Union)	47,545	0.9	0.1
Baptist	26,425	0.5	0.1
Friends	10,570	0.2	—
Methodist	7,140	0.1	—
Presbyterian	5,650	0.1	—
Other Church Related	66,519	1.3	0.1
Nonchurch Related	370,836	7.0	0.7

Source: President's Panel on Nonpublic Education, *Nonpublic Education and the Public Good* (Washington: U.S. Government Printing Office, 1972), pp. 6-7. Public school enrollment from NEA, *Estimates of School Statistics, 1971-72*, Research Report 1971-R13 (Washington: NEA Research Division, 1971), p. 10.

Nonpublic enrollments are concentrated in these states, and more generally in the North and East, for a number of reasons.[c] First, Catholics in general are concentrated in these areas of the country, and, as noted earlier, enrollments in Catholic schools are the largest element of nonpublic enrollments. In addition, these states tend to be among the more densely populated ones. Other things equal, a nonpublic school that has to compete for enrollments will have a larger market from which to draw in a more densely populated area.[d] Moreover, a state's density also reflects its degree of urbanization, and the quality and racial composition of large city public schools leads a number of people to seek nonpublic schooling. The distribution of nonpublic school students among the states is also affected by the relative wealth of the respective states—other things equal, wealthier people can afford more nonpublic education. Finally, the older states that

[c]Observed enrollment at any point in time represents the intersection of aggregate demand and aggregate supply. For a more complete discussion of the factors underlying both demand and supply, particularly at the individual level, see pages 26-37.

[d]Note that by law public schools are required to serve all areas of the country.

Table 2-2

Nonpublic School Enrollment as Percentage of Total Enrollment, Selected States, 1970-71 School Year

State of Local Government	Percentage of Total School Enrollment in Nonpublic Schools
States with High Fraction of Students in Nonpublic Schools	
Rhode Island	19.3
Pennsylvania	19.2
New York	18.8
New Jersey	18.3
Wisconsin	18.2
Illinois	16.9
Massachusetts	16.3
States with Low Fraction of Students in Nonpublic Schools	
Alabama	4.0
Georgia	3.1
Alaska	2.8
Arkansas	2.7
Oklahoma	2.5
North Carolina	2.4
Utah	2.0

Source: U.S. Bureau of the Census, *Census of Population: 1970 General Social and Economic Characteristics,* Final Report, PC(1)-C (volumes for the respective states).

are concentrated in the North and East tend to have a long tradition of nonpublic schooling, especially of non-Catholic schools.[e] While enrollments in such schools are as high as 7.6 percent in the New England states, they are often less than 1 percent in southern and western states.[2]

A simple regression using 1970 data found that these four factors accounted for five-sixths of the variation in the states' nonpublic elementary school enrollments, with Catholic population being the most important factor:[3]

$$\text{Log } E = 42.14 + 0.49 \text{ Log } C + 0.21 \text{ Log } D + 0.51 \text{ Log } Y$$
$$(0.06) \qquad (0.05) \qquad (0.35)$$

$$- 6.17 \text{ Log } A, \qquad (2.1)$$
$$(2.03)$$

$$R^2 = 0.83$$

---

[e]Remember that public schools did not begin to become commonplace until after the Civil War.

E = % enrolled in nonpublic schools

C = % of population which is Catholic

D = Densely in population per square mile

Y = Per capita income

A = Year of admission to the union

(Standard error in parentheses)

Within most states, moreover, the nonpublic school enrollments show a disproportionate urban bias; they are over one-and-a-half times more concentrated in central cities than are public schools, and Catholic school enrollments are over twice as concentrated (Table 2-4). As Table 2-3

Table 2-3
Nonpublic Enrollment in Selected States and Cities, 1970-71

	Total Nonpublic Enrollment	As percentage of Total School Enrollment
New York	789,110	18.8
New York City	379,946	25.9
Buffalo	28,573	29.4
Pennsylvania	514,853	19.2
Philadelphia	146,298	35.5
Pittsburgh	37,155	34.9
Illinois	451,724	16.9
Chicago	208,174	27.2
California	378,531	8.3
Los Angeles	71,606	12.6
San Francisco	29,582	23.8
Ohio	347,789	14.8
Cleveland	33,876	17.8
Cincinnati	23,535	21.8
New Jersey	325,208	18.3
Michigan	285,862	13.2
Detroit	62,225	21.9
Massachusetts	227,621	16.3
Boston	37,237	29.1
Total, 8 States	3,320,698	16.3
Total, 11 Cities	1,058,207	26.5

Sources: President's Panel on Nonpublic Education, Final Report, *Nonpublic Education and the Public Good* (Washington: U.S. Government Printing Office, 1972), pp. 15, 18; and U.S. Bureau of the Census, *Census of Population,* PC(1)-C (volumes for the respective states), Tables 51 and 83.

showed, in many large cities, more than one-fourth of all students attend nonpublic schools. Moreover, Catholic enrollments are becoming more concentrated in cities while public school enrollments are becoming less so. While over 21 percent of all Catholic schools outside the central cities shut down between 1967 and 1973, only 13 percent of the central city schools closed.[4] The difference between total nonpublic figures and the Catholic figures (Table 2-3) suggests that non-Catholic nonpublic schools are concentrated in suburban areas.

The one deviation from this pattern is the South where "white academies" have been set up to avoid forced desegregation. While nonpublic enrollments in these states remain a small percentage of the total, in a few communities and counties they represent a substantial fraction. Noxubee County, Mississippi, for example, has nearly 22 percent of its students in nonpublic schools; for the town of Canton the figure is over 41 percent.[5]

Turning to the finances of the nonpublic schools, there is indeed substantial diversity. Expenditure levels in the nonpublic schools vary nearly as much as those in the nation's public schools. Catholic schools in 1970-71 and 1973-74 spent on average less than 40 percent of the public school average per pupil (Table 2-5).[f] Other sectarian schools, especially the Lutheran, did not fare much better. On the other extreme, the Episcopal schools and the mostly nonsectarian schools affiliated with the National Association of Independent Schools spent at levels comparable to the highest public school districts in the country. Variations within the Catholic sector itself were equally substantial. While some Catholic elementary schools, for example, spent as little as $100 per pupil in 1971-72, others spent over $1500.[6]

There are two principal reasons why the reported Catholic and Lutheran expenditure levels are "artificially" low. First, these schools receive large amounts of "contributed services" from faculty. Members of religious orders, who comprise about one-half of Catholic school staffs, are paid only subsistence wages; and the lay faculty receive on average only about 80 percent of their public school counterparts (the difference being an implicit contribution to the church).[7] The second factor is the large amount of "off-the-budget financing" done by these schools. Often administrative and maintenance services appear only on the books of the supporting church. Moreover, these schools receive a number of in-kind services from the various governments, such as transportation, textbooks, and health services, which do not appear in their expenditure records.[g]

The remaining differences are the result of these schools being operated

[f]Since Catholic schools tend to be concentrated in areas with high-spending public schools, real differences are even more substantial.

[g]Many states have strict constitutions restricting aid to nonpublic schools. Hence programs are actually administered by the local public school. This is also true for federal programs such as Title I of ESEA.

Table 2-4

Distribution of Public and Nonpublic School Enrollment, by Location, Fall 1972 (Percentage)

Location	Public School Enroll- ment	Total Nonpublic School Enrollment	Catholic School Enroll- ment	Nonpublic Enrollment as a Fraction of Total School Enrollment
Central City	27.2	41.4	52.7	14.8
Suburbs	38.5	41.8	29.9	11.1
Small Town and Rural	34.2	16.8	17.4	5.3
All Schools	100.0	100.0	100.0	10.2

Sources: Public and nonpublic enrollment from U.S. Bureau of the Census, *Current Population Reports*, Series P-20, no. 260, Social and Economic Characteristics of Students: October 1972 (1974), Table 3, p.22; Catholic data from NCEA, *U.S. Catholic Schools, 1973-74*, p. 9.

Table 2-5

Average per Pupil Expenditures in Selected Types of Nonpublic Schools, and in Public Schools, 1970-71 and 1973-74 School Years (Amounts in Dollars)

Type of School	Average per Pupil Cost	
	1970-71	1973-74
Nonpublic		
Roman Catholic	307	419
Elementary	240	346
Secondary	532	647
Lutheran	410	475
Episcopal	1,320	—
Jewish	990	—
National Association of Independent Schools	1,781	1,884
Other Nonpublic	600	—
Public	812	1,048

Sources: Catholic data from NCEA, *U.S. Catholic Schools, 1970-71*, pp. 9, 10, 27; and *U.S. Catholic Schools, 1973-74*, pp 22-25; Lutheran data from Al H. Senske, "Lutheran School Statistics, 1971-72," Board of Parish Education, Lutheran Church-Missouri Synod (St. Louis: Board, 1972; processed); and "School Statistics of the Lutheran Church—Missouri Synod, September 1973," table 26; NAIS data from *NAIS Report*, no. 39 (January 1972), pp. 2, 10, and NAIS Report no. 49 (February 1974), pp. 11-13 (using day-school data only); public data from National Education Association, *Estimates of School Statistics, 1971-72*, p. 36, and NEA, Estimates of School Statistics, 1973-74, p 35; other groups are authors' estimates based on data in Arthur J. Corazzini, "The Non-Catholic Private School," in Frank J. Fahey, director, *Economic Problems of Nonpublic Schools*, Submitted to the President's Commission on School Finance by the Office for Educational Research, University of Notre Dame (Washington: Commission, 1972).

with fewer inputs than their public counterparts. In Catholic schools, for example, classes tend to be larger than in the public schools (see Table 2-6). Also these schools tend to have far less in the way of high-cost facilities such as laboratories, industrial shops, or athletic facilities.

There is also tremendous variation in the reliance that the different nonpublic schools place on various sources of revenue. While Catholic and Lutheran schools, for example, derive less than half of their income from tuition and fees,[8] the NAIS schools obtain nearly 80 percent of their revenues from this source (Table 2-6). Average tuition and fees in Catholic schools is only one-eighth that of the NAIS schools. The low tuitions in Catholic schools are an effort to make these schools quasi-public in nature—the Catholic position is that no child should be excluded from a school because his or her family is unable to afford the tuition.[9]

As an alternative to tuition, Catholic and other religiously affiliated schools rely heavily on church subsidies. Aside from maintaining the quasi-public nature of these schools, this method of financing is desirable for tax reasons. While tuition payments are not tax-deductible, contributions to churches are. Hence in recent years Catholic parishes have tended to add special collections and to exert pressure on Catholic school parents to make larger contributions in lieu of tuition.[10]

Other sources of income to the nonpublic schools are much less important. Private gifts and endowments, although the second largest source of funds for the NAIS schools, are still only a small fraction; and this source is virtually insignificant for the Catholic schools. Similarly, government revenues are not a very large fraction of nonpublic school budgets. In 1972-73, direct aid from state and local governments accounted for 2.2 percent of Catholic school income.[h] For the NAIS schools such aid was negligible. Similarly federal government funds accounted for about 2 percent of Catholic schools income, and an even smaller amount for other nonpublic schools. Almost half this money is aid for disadvantaged students (ESEA, Title I); another third is from the national school lunch programs, and the remainder is mostly aid provided under federal supplementary services and library resources programs. Most of the recent growth in federal assistance has resulted not from new programs, but from the schools taking advantage of programs for which they were already eligible. As noted earlier, one reason reported revenues from public sources are so low is that much government aid is in-kind and hence off the budget. (See Chapter 5 for a more complete discussion of current public assistance.)

The Shifting Equilibrium—Declining Enrollments

Over the last six years, nonpublic enrollment has been steadily declining,

[h]This aid includes a variety of "child-benefit" services such as health and transportation. It

almost entirely as a result of declines in Catholic enrollment (Table 2-7). The 1973 total is nearly 30 percent below its 1965 counterpart. Since 1964 Catholic school enrollments have declined at more than 200,000 students per year, or an annual rate of nearly 4 percent. Most of this decline has taken place in the elementary schools, whose enrollments are down nearly 40 percent from their peak of 4.5 million.[11] During the same period, Catholic secondary enrollment declined only 17 percent.[12]

Non-Catholic nonpublic school enrollment has actually been increasing slightly in recent years. In fact, since 1961 there has been an increase in enrollments in both other religiously affiliated schools and in nonaffiliated schools and there has been a net increase in every region of the country (Table 2-8). This is not to say that Catholics are alone in their decline. Lutheran elementary schools and Mennonite institutions among the other religious schools, and boarding schools and military academies among the nonaffiliated[13] have all experienced declines. Moreover, most of the growth among those schools which did increase took place in the early part of the decade; and enrollments in these schools have now begun to level off. The elite NAIS schools have actually had small declines in recent years. And, in fact, since 1967, total non-Catholic nonpublic enrollment has only increased 3.1 percent (Table 2-7).

The decline in Catholic enrollments has taken place in every region, although it has been somewhat larger in the Midwest. Moreover, as noted earlier, it has been concentrated in suburban and rural areas. While it is difficult, due to lack of data, to say where exactly the increases in other nonpublic schools have occurred, it is possible that much of it has occurred in the large central cities. In New York City, for example, where many people believe that the public schools have seriously deteriorated, there has been a substantial increase in non-Catholic nonpublic enrollment.[14] Table 2-8 would also seem to verify the stories about rapid growth of southern "white academies." While in certain locales these schools represent a sizable fraction of total enrollments, the overall importance should not be exaggerated. A study done on Mississippi by the Southeastern Public Education Project, and largely corroborated by a Justice Department staff report, [15] suggests that probably 15,000 to 20,000 students have left public schools in the last three years to attend these academies. However, this represents only a little over 3 percent of total Mississippi school enrollment.

In sum, the declines in nonpublic school enrollment have been concentrated among a few groups. While not exclusively Catholic, explaining the declines in Catholic schools is a useful surrogate for explaining declines in the whole sector, first because they account for virtually all of the decline, and secondly because the factors affecting them are similar to those affect-

---

also includes aid for such things as textbooks, remedial instruction, and various testing and record-keeping activities required by the state.

Table 2-6

Revenue per Pupil of Selected Nonpublic Elementary and Secondary Schools, by Source, 1972-73 School Year (Amounts in Dollars)

Source of Revenue	Catholic Schools		Lutheran Schools		National Association of Independent Schools	
	Per Pupil	Percentage	Per Pupil	Percentage	Per Pupil	Percentage
Tuition and Fees	178	46.1	134	28.3	1500	79.6
Gifts and Endowments	8	2.0	31	6.6	222	11.8
Church Subsidies	166	42.8	296	62.2	—0—	—0—
Government Assistance	15	4.0	12	2.5	11	0.6
Other	20	5.1	2	0.4	151	8.0
Total	387	100.0	475	100.0	1884	100.0

Sources: Same as for Catholic, Lutheran and NAIS data in Table 2-5. NAIS data are for day schools only.

Table 2-7
School-Age Population and Enrollment in Nonpublic Elementary and Secondary Schools, Fall 1960-1973 (Thousands)

Year	Total School-Age Population	Total Catholic School-Age Population	Total Enrollment in Nonpublic Schools	Enrollment in Catholic Schools	Enrollment in Other Nonpublic Schools	Nonpublic as Percentage of Total School Enrollment
1960	44,189	8,374	5,969	5,254	715	14.0
1961	45,303	8,713	6,011	5,370	641	13.7
1962	46,698	9,051	6,003	5,494	509	13.5
1963	48,005	9,385	6,397	5,591	806	13.9
1964	49,536	9,712	6,732	5,601	1,131	14.3
1965	49,995	10,121	6,953	5,574	1,379	14.3
1966	50,836	10,250	6,671	—	—	13.5
1967	51,584	10,378	6,489	5,198	1,291	12.8
1968	52,272	10,539	6,145	4,941	1,204	12.0
1969	52,787	10,656	5,711	4,658	1,053	11.1
1970	53,039	10,720	5,655	4,364	1,292	10.9
1971	52,266	10,720	5,378	4,035	1,343	10.4
1972	51,819	10,603	5,203	3,790	1,413	10.2
1973	51,375	10,397	4,945	3,614	1,331	9.9

Sources: Total nonpublic enrollment from U.S. Bureau of the Census, *Current Population Reports*, Series P-20, no. 261, "School Enrollment in the United States: October 1973" (1974), p. 3, and preceding issues for 1960-64; National Catholic Educational Association, *A Statistical Report on Catholic Elementary and Secondary Schools for the Years 1967-68 to 1969-70* (Washington: NCEA Research Department, 1970), pp. 5, 8; NCEA, *U.S. Catholic Schools, 1973-74* p. 9; total school-age population from NEA *Estimates of School Statistics, 1973-74*, p. 8; Catholic school-age population from Kenneth M. Brown, "Enrollment in Nonpublic Schools," in Fahey, *Nonpublic Schools*, p. 160.

Table 2-8
Percentage Change in Nonpublic School Enrollment, 1961-2 to 1970-71, by Region and Affiliation

	Catholic	Other Religious	Nonaffiliated
North Atlantic	−14.5	44.5	28.7
Great Lakes and Plains	−21.8	26.4	110.7
Southeast	−5.6	167.7	242.4
West and Southwest	−18.0	39.6	80.5
U.S. Total	−17.0	48.9	92.9

Source: U.S. Department of Health, Education, and Welfare, *NCES Bulletin*, no. 12, June 7, 1972.

ing the other declining groups—and it is likely that many of these factors may yet affect other affiliated schools which are still maintaining enrollments. Explaining the factors underlying the demand and supply of Catholic schools may provide some insight into why other types of nonpublic schools have not experienced large declines.

The cause for decline that has been given the most attention in the current public debate is rising costs. As Table 2-9 clearly points out, costs in the Catholic schools have been rising at a very rapid rate. During the period 1967-68 to 1972-73, while public school costs were rising less than one-half, Catholic elementary expenditures well more than doubled and Catholic secondary went up by nearly four-fifths.

Three sources of rapid growth in Catholic schools costs have been the steady shift from religious to lay teachers, the decline in pupil teacher ratios, and the rise in faculty salaries. The shift to lay teachers has been forced on the Catholic schools by the rapid decline in vocations to Catholic religious orders in recent years, and by these orders broadening their missions to include other than teaching activities. In the 1967-73 period alone, the percentage of lay teachers in the elementary schools rose from 41 to 60 percent, and in the secondary schools from 38 to 57 percent.[16] However, as Table 2-10 shows, the changing mix of teachers accounted for only one-ninth of the increase in Catholic elementary school costs. The second factor, falling pupil-teacher ratios, accounted for about one-sixth of the recent increases. In part, the decline in these ratios was involuntary, a result of the Catholic schools being unable to fill their classrooms and hence operating at less than capacity. In part, however, the decline also reflects an effort to improve quality in response to pressure from parents and to reduce workload in response to pressure from teachers.[17] Despite the recent reduction, pupil-teacher ratios in Catholic elementary schools still exceed those in the public sector.

The rapid rise in salaries appears to have been the principal factor in the

Table 2-9

Comparison of per Pupil Costs, Teachers' Salaries, and Pupil/Teacher Ratios, Catholics and Public Schools, 1967-68 to 1972-73 School Years

Item	1967-68	1972-73	Percentage Change, 1967-72
Per Pupil Cost			
Catholic Elementary	$ 145	$ 315	117.2
Catholic Secondary	335	601	79.4
Public Elementary and Secondary	658	968	47.1
Average Teacher Salary			
Catholic Elementary (Lay)	$4,246	6,351	49.6
Catholic Elementary (Religious)	1,285	—	—
Catholic Secondary (Lay)	6,138	8,525	38.9
Catholic Secondary (Religious)	1,285	—	55.3
Public Elementary	7,280	9,876	35.7
Public Secondary	7,692	10,497	36.5
Pupil/Teacher Ratios			
Catholic Elementary	33.4	27.2	−18.6
Catholic Secondary	20.0	18.2	−9.0
Public Elementary	26.2	23.5	−10.3
Public Secondary	20.5	19.3	−5.9

Sources: Catholic data from NCEA, *Catholic Elementary and Secondary Schools, 1967-68 to 1969-70,* and NCEA, *U.S. Catholic Schools, 1973-74;* public school data from NEA, *Estimates of School Statistics, 1973-74.*

cost increases. The salaries of both religious and lay teachers have risen at a faster rate than those of their public school counterparts.[18] In part, this increase is the result of a relative improvement in the qualifications of Catholic school teachers: the number of teachers without B.A. degrees has been substantially reduced in recent years.[19] More important, though, has been Catholic school teachers becoming increasingly more militant and organized. In New York, San Francisco, and other archdioceses where teachers are now represented by unions affiliated with the AFL-CIO, teachers have actually struck for better pay and working conditions, rejecting the notion that they should make a large implicit contribution to the church. Their bargaining strategy has been to attempt to tie their wages to the neighboring public-school schedules. In many places they have succeeded in obtaining 90 percent of parity or more, although Catholic administrators have sought to lessen the impact of such bargaining by hiring less educated and experienced teachers.[20]

Taken together, the three factors—all of which are actually part of the per pupil cost of instructional personnel—account for three-fifths of the

Table 2-10

Increase in per Pupil Costs of Catholic Elementary and Public Schools, by Source, 1967-68 to 1972-73 School Years (Amounts in Dollars)

Source of Increase	Amount of Increase Dollars per Pupil		As Percentage of Total Change in Cost		As Percentage of per Pupil Cost, 1967	
	Catholic Schools	Public Schools	Catholic Schools	Public Schools	Catholic Schools	Public Schools
Total	170.00	310.00	100.0	100.0	117.2	47.1
Shift to Lay	19.56		11.5		13.5	
Salary Rise	55.48	107.70	32.6	34.8	38.3	16.4
Lower Pupil/Teacher	28.56	40.45	16.8	13.0	19.7	6.1
Price Increases and More Materials and Service	66.40	161.85	39.1	52.2	45.8	24.6

Sources: NCEA, *Catholic Elementary and Secondary Schools, 1967-68 to 1969-70*, and NCEA, *U.S. Catholic Schools, 1973-74*; public school data computed from NEA, *Estimates of School Statistics, 1973-74*.

increase in per pupil costs in Catholic elementary schools (Table 2-10).[1] The balance of the increase was the result of rising prices and the provision of additional materials and services.

Such increases in costs shift the supply curve in two ways: raising prices (i.e., tuition and fees) or closing schools.[j] There are a number of institutional barriers to cost increases being translated into a shift in supply through either means. First, the Catholic elementary schools have always been conceived of as a quasi-public system (see Chapter 1), and raising tuitions is viewed as a move away from such a system. In addition, parish officials are hesitant to raise tuitions because the debate on public aid has convinced many that both Catholic school parents and the church or religious orders are incapable of providing the additional sums and that any increase in tuition will cause serious enrollment reductions.[21] Moreover, church leaders have convinced their members that the schools are important, and any proposal for closing the schools, even as part of a consolidation program, must be seen as a manifestation of the system's collapse. Parish pastors frequently support this view because they are reluctant to consolidate their underutilized schools with those of neighboring parishes and hence yield some of their power and authority. In lieu of price increases or closing schools, Catholic school officials have incurred substantial operating deficits in recent years,[k] with the hope that new sources of public or private funds will be found to pay off these debts.

Considering first the effect of cost increases on prices, Table 2-11 shows what has happened to average Catholic school revenues over the last five years. As the table indicates, tuition and fees in Catholic schools have actually increased at a faster rate than expenditures in both elementary and secondary schools. Particularly in the elementary schools, these rapid increases are the result of the very slow growth in general church revenues—although parish subsidies to schools, for example, fell as a fraction of total school revenue, these subsidies increased from 36 percent of parish revenues in 1965 to 53 percent in 1970.[22]

Although the percentage rate of growth in tuition and fees at Catholic elementary schools has been quite high in recent years, the absolute amounts have been small, and hence tuition and fees remain extremely low.

---

[i]The higher rates of increase in these costs in Catholic schools relative to the public schools also account for virtually all of the relatively higher increases in total Catholic school costs.

[j]In standard economic theory, shutdowns are not in themselves part of a shift in supply. Rather, cost increases are passed on in the form of higher prices; if demand is insufficient, the resulting cutback in output may include some firms closing. Catholic schools, however, do not automatically pass on cost increases. Many, for reasons discussed below, are unwilling to raise prices and simply close (e.g., in New York State thirty of the 76 schools which closed between 1965 and 1969 charged no tuition at all). Hence "school closings" are a very integral part of the reduction in supply.

[k]In 1970-71 the total operating deficit for Catholic schools was over $750 million.

Table 2-11

Change in Income per Pupil, Catholic Elementary and Secondary Schools, by Source, 1967-68 to 1972-73 School Years (Amounts in Dollars)

Source of Income	Amount of Income, 1972-73	Percentage of Total	Percentage Change, 1967-72
		Elementary	
Total	315	100.0	117.2
Tuition	90	28.6	177.1
Fees	15	4.8	59.1
Parish Subsidy	162	51.4	88.1
Diocesan Subsidy	4	1.3	119.8
Other	44	14.0	186.3
		Secondary	
Total Income	601	100.0	79.4
Tuition	394	65.6	116.2
Fees	40	6.6	89.5
Parish Subsidy	48	8.0	7.7
Diocesan Subsidy	45	7.5	106.6
Other	74	12.3	13.3

Sources: National Catholic Educational Association, *A Statistical Report on Catholic Elementary and Secondary Schools for the Years 1967-68 to 1969-70,* and NCEA, *A Report on U.S. Catholic Schools, 1973-74.*

The 150 percent growth in tuition and fees actually represented an increase of only $63 per student, the 1972-73 level equaling $105. This increase covered only 37 percent of the increases in costs. Even if it is assumed that Catholic school parents pay all of the "parish subsidy,"[1] the 1972-73 total payment was $267, only $70 higher than in 1967-68.[m] Compared to the growth in the average Catholic family's income, these increases were quite small.

Catholic secondary tuitions and fees are considerably higher than those for elementary schools, principally because these schools do not receive the substantial church subsidies which support the elementary schools.[n] Although tuition and fees have risen some $230 over the last three years, at

---

[1] As noted earlier, in parishes with low school tuitions, pressure is put on parents to contribute; in some cases such contributions are effectively made mandatory.

[m] While the data is presented here in terms of average cost per student, Catholic and other sectarian schools frequently charge by the family or give discounts to students with an older brother or sister in the school. Also some schools do use discriminatory pricing, varying tuition with family income—much in the quasi-public spirit of these schools (see "NCEA standard School Survey Form (1972)"). However, it is much more common to seek larger payments from more affluent families in their church contributions.

[n] Catholic secondary schools do not have the same "quasi-public" tradition that the elementary schools have. In line with this difference, while some allowance is made for scholarships, very little use is made of discriminatory pricing.

$430 they are still well below the tuitions charged by most other nonpublic secondary schools.

The impact that these price increases have had on Catholic school enrollments depends on the price elasticity of demand for Catholic schooling, over the relevant range of prices. Although the available data is somewhat sketchy, analysis of it strongly suggests that, at current levels of tuition, demand for Catholic elementary school education is highly inelastic. Using a simple model of demand and supply, and data on prices and enrollments in two periods for each of nearly 800 Catholic schools, demand curves were estimated separately for the elementary and the secondary schools by means of linear regression analysis. (Discussion of the data used and the analysis done is contained in Appendix 2A.) While the coefficients of determination were low for all regression equations, the price coefficients in each were highly significant (see this chapter's Appendix 2A). Evaluating the equations at average tuition levels, it is estimated that the price elasticity of demand was between -0.04 and -0.07 for the typical elementary school and between -0.09 and -0.18 for the typical secondary school.

A variety of other studies tends to confirm this result. Analysis of changes in tuition and enrollment for a sample of 103 schools in St. Louis found no significant relationship.[23] A similar study of 15 schools in Atlanta found no relationship.[24] The Fleishman Commission, in studying New York State, concluded that "there is no evidence . . . that tuition increases have significantly effected enrollment."[25] The Gurash Committee in Philadelphia concluded similarly that the "evidence to date, and at the levels of tuition now charged, seems to indicate that the demand for Catholic school education is insensitive to current tuition levels."[26] Kenneth Brown, after reviewing a number of studies for the President's Commission and calculating an elasticity of aggregate demand, concluded that "it would be hard to argue that any other estimate is more accurate than something in the range of -0.05 to -0.15."[27] In terms of traditional economic theory, this evidence suggests that either the substitution effect or the income effect, or both, must be small. That the former is small seems reasonable because schooling is considered a "necessity" and many Catholic families perceive no substitutes for Catholic schooling. (For a discussion of how this is changing, see below.) The income effect is also likely to be small for many Catholic families because tuitions in many Catholic schools represent a very small part of the families' budgets.

In view of the tremendous percentage increases in tuition and fees in Catholic elementary schools in recent years (see Table 2-11), these estimates imply that between 20 and 40 percent of the decline in Catholic elementary school enrollments may be attributed to a rise in price. A point estimate at the average tuition level suggests that one-third is probably a best estimate. In other words, rises in tuition and fees have caused about

80,000 elementary students a year to transfer to the public school system. Similarly, an estimate for secondary schools suggests that about three-fifths or nearly 20,000 students a year have left these schools because of increases in price.

The second result of increased costs is the closings of schools. In recent years the oft-heard statement that, "Catholic schools are closing at a rate of one a day," is actually an underestimate. From 1967 to 1973 there was an average annual decline of 300 elementary schools and 93 secondary schools.[28] These schools closed, essentially, when increases in revenue were insufficient to cover cost increases. As noted earlier, institutional barriers frequently prevented a sufficient rise in prices, despite the high inelasticity of demand, when other revenue sources were not available.[o]

It is estimated that the schools which did close between 1967 and 1973 enrolled 360,000 elementary students and 130,000 secondary students.[29] Not all of these closings, however, directly forced students to transfer to the public schools—that is, reflect a reduction in supply. There has been some consolidation which did not produce a net reduction in the number of places available.[30] As many as 36,000 elementary students were consolidated from parochial to interparochial or diocesan schools. Another 24,000 to 48,000 students may have been absorbed into neighboring parish schools.[31] Of the remaining, some would have left anyway, as they did schools that remained opened—if these schools were typical, about 50,000 students would have transferred on their own. Hence reductions in supply through the closing of Catholic elementary schools from 1967 to 1973 caused the total enrollment decline to increase by 13 to 15 percent. A comparable figure for the secondary schools is harder to estimate because attendance patterns for these schools are much less clear. However, these schools are also much less important, as only 10 percent of Catholic school enrollment decline occurred in the high schools. Using similar assumptions as for the elementary schools,[p] it is estimated that 60,000 secondary students were forced to transfer to public schools because of school closings—that is, school closings account for 32 percent of the net decline in Catholic secondary school enrollment.

---

[o]While tuition increases can *cause* schools to close, because of generally highly inelastic demand and the generally low tuitions in schools which did close, the overlap of these two sources of reduction in supply is assumed to be negligible.

Institutional barriers also frequently prevented the necessary consolidation to hold down large increases in per pupil costs resulting from underutilization. However, in the absence of a mechanism for fully passing on those cost increases to students still enrolled, it is arbitrary whether such a school closing should be counted as a reduction in supply or as demand induced. For simplicity, all students forced to transfer to public schools as a result of such a closing are counted on the supply side—note that double-counting is avoided by treating demand as a residual.

[p]A calculation as in note 24 yields 58,000 students absorbed into neighboring schools (assumes *all* schools had another school sufficiently nearby); it was assumed that no schools were consolidated and that 12,000 students would have transferred had the schools remained open.

School closings taken together with tuition increases, then, account for a little less than half of the total recent decline in Catholic school enrollments. The remaining half, then, must have been the result of a decline in demand. A priori we would expect the level of any individual's demand for Catholic schooling at a given price to be a function of the perceived relative substitutability of other goods, wealth, and tastes. Summing these demands over Catholics with school-age children would give us the aggregate demand for Catholic schooling. The substitute for Catholic schooling is the local public school—the choice a parent makes at any point in time is not continuous but rather binary, either send the child to Catholic school or to public school. The nominal price for public school is zero; the parent's tax liability would not change if they were to transfer their children. However, to the extent that the public school's perceived quality is greater or less than the Catholic school, or the extent to which its perceived relative quality changes, its real price may be thought to be greater or less than zero. Hence we should expect that families who live in neighborhoods with better public schools (e.g., suburbs) will enroll their children in Catholic schools at a lower rate than families in poorer neighborhoods. On the other hand, to the extent that the parents perceive Catholic schooling to be something different from public schooling, the public school may be thought less of a substitute.[q]

Turning to the effects of wealth, one might expect positive income effects in the demand for nonpublic schooling—higher income families can better afford such schooling. However, these effects might not show up statistically because high-income people tend to be concentrated in neighborhoods where they have access to better public schools than do poorer Catholic families—that is, they face a lower real price of public schooling, and it may be that the substitution effect is stronger than the income effect.

Two elements of taste are important in the demand for Catholic schooling. First, the strength of a parent's attachment to the institutional church determines how substitutable he or she views Catholic and public education, or what value the parent attaches to the Catholic part of his child's schooling. Second, the parent's level of own education plays a significant role in determining how important quality of instruction is for its child.

National data is unavailable to estimate the importance of each, or all, of these factors. However, one study done on the St. Louis Metropolitan area (which is in many ways representative of Catholic schooling nationally), found the following results:[32]

---

[q]Put another way, Catholic schools may be viewed as providing secular services (similar to public schools) plus the teaching of religion. The price parents pay in tuition is actually for this latter service (plus or minus any net difference in the quality of secular services provided by the Catholic and public schools respectively). If the role of religion in Catholic schools diminishes (or if the relative quality of their secular services are lower), we should expect parents to be willing to pay less.

For elementary schools,

$$Q = \underset{(0.243)}{0.865} + \underset{(0.004)}{0.013A} - \underset{(0.009)}{0.037E} - \underset{(0.094)}{0.142H} + \underset{(0.026)}{0.025F}$$

$$+ \underset{(0.0008)}{0.0003N} - \underset{(0.0001)}{0.00046} - \underset{(0.150)}{0.666R}, \tag{2.2}$$

$$R^2 = 0.82$$

$$Q = \underset{(0.249)}{0.449} + \underset{(0.004)}{0.015A} - \underset{(0.005)}{0.014Y} + \underset{(0.098)}{0.116H} + \underset{(0.028)}{0.031F}$$

$$+ \underset{(0.0008)}{0.0004N} - \underset{(0.0001)}{0.0004C} - \underset{(0.152)}{0.146R}, \tag{2.3}$$

$$R^2 = 0.80$$

For secondary schools,

$$Q = \underset{(0.348)}{-0.067} + \underset{(0.005)}{0.001A} + \underset{(0.011)}{0.021E} - \underset{(0.130)}{0.133H} - \underset{(0.032)}{0.024F}$$

$$+ \underset{(0.0010)}{0.0006N} - \underset{(0.178)}{0.686R}, \tag{2.4}$$

$$R^2 = 0.63$$

$$Q = \underset{(0.337)}{0.223} + \underset{(0.005)}{0.009A} + \underset{(0.006)}{0.013Y} - \underset{(0.130)}{0.164H} + \underset{(0.038)}{0.012F}$$

$$+ \underset{(0.0010)}{0.0005N} - \underset{(0.175)}{0.679R}, \tag{2.5}$$

$$R^2 = 0.63$$

Where Q = % of a parish who enroll their children in Catholic schools,

        A = mean age of family head,

        E = mean level of parent's education,

        Y = mean level of parent's income,

        H = % who owned homes,

        F = mean family size,

        N = % nonwhite in parish,

C = current expenditures in parish school (more an indication of school location than of quality, since low-cost religious teachers tend to be concentrated in poorer areas),

and

R = % of parents who could not enroll their child because school was full.

These results tend to verify our a priori theory, both as to the important factors and the direction of their impact. While data is again unavailable from which to estimate by how much changes in these factors may have caused aggregate demand to shift, there is considerable evidence to support the assertion that it has declined markedly—that the important factors affecting demand have changed significantly in the appropriate directions.

In recent years, Catholics have "caught up" with the nation as a whole in terms of their income distribution. As more and more of them have reached middle- and upper-income levels, and as more of them have received more extensive education,[33] they have, like their non-Catholic counterparts, begun to place more emphasis on the education of their children.[r] They are no longer satisfied with the large class sizes, the numbers of teachers without advanced training, and the lack of facilities necessitated by the very tight budgets of Catholic schools mentioned earlier. Also like their non-Catholic counterparts, many of these parents have moved to the suburbs[s] where the choice is no longer between a deteriorating public institution and a nearby parish school, but rather between a good neighborhood public school with extensive facilities and a possibly distant Catholic school with few "extras." A number of surveys have found that suburban Catholics perceive their local public schools to be academically superior to Catholic schools, in contrast to Catholics in the central cities.[34] A survey of the Catholic laity in the suburbs of the Archdiocese of Indianapolis, which asked whether the local public school or Catholic school better prepared students for college and for a job, found the following results (expressed of all respondents):[35]

	Public School Is Better	Catholic School Is Better	No Difference
Preparation for College	37.9% (8.7)	15.7% (38.4)	38.9% (40.0)
Preparation for Job	42.2% (22.8)	6.9% (26.7)	44.4% (40.0)

[r]Note that these are precisely the parents who are best prepared to do this instructing themselves. Note also that this change in tastes offsets these parents' increased ability to afford nonpublic schooling.

[s]This suburbanization has depopulated a number of inner-city parishes, forcing them to close their schools for lack of children.

In the St. Louis area, while the fraction of suburban Catholic children attending Catholic schools declined by 15 to 20 percent over the last few years, the fraction of Catholic children in the city of St. Louis attending Catholic schools has actually risen by 8 percent.[36]

Thus, while one would expect that higher incomes would enable parents to better afford Catholic schooling and hence to demand more of it, increased incomes also enable these parents to move to neighborhoods where the competing public schools are the best and the Catholic school perhaps less accessible. As Dugan's study showed, the result on the impact of income is mixed.[t]

In addition to the effects of changing incomes, for a variety of reasons the public schools have become a more viable alternative for ever-increasing numbers of Catholic parents. Catholic schools were originally founded in the country in the late nineteenth century because of the strong Protestant bias in the public schools (see Chapter 1). Such a bias no longer exists and hence Catholic parents are much less apprehensive about sending their children to public schools. From the other side, moreover, as the numbers of religious instructors have declined and as discipline has been relaxed in the Catholic schools, they have begun to lose their distinctive character and to look more and more like the public schools. The Second Vatican Council, which created a more liberal atmosphere within the church, has tended to reinforce these trends. The council emphasized that parents are principally responsible for the religious education of their children.[37] As Catholics have become better educated, and hence better equipped to assume this responsibility, they have less and less found a need to utilize church schools. Some priests and other church leaders have encouraged this shift away from parochial schools as a means of revitalizing the parish community. Conscious of the emphasis the Second Vatican Council has placed on lay participation, they have reasoned that the parish should place less emphasis on school—in many parishes this is the only activity—and more in involving the adult community in church activities.[38]

Finally, the increased substitutability may be a product of the diminishing role that organized religion is playing for all Americans, particularly Catholics. In the last seven years, the percentage of all adults attending church on any Sunday fell from 45 to 40; during the same period, the percentage of Catholics attending Mass fell from 71 to 57. As parents become less involved in organized religion, it is likely they place less

---

[t]"Income" was negatively related to Catholic school enrollment at the elementary level and positively related at the secondary level; see pp. 33-35 and note 27. One reason for this difference is that Catholic secondary schools generally offer only college preparatory programs, which may increase their perceived relative quality for some parents. The positive impact of income shown in equation 2.1 suggests that for non-Catholic nonpublic schools, income has a significant positive effect—the low significance level for the income coefficient, however, is likely the result of this "mixed" effect. The positive coefficient also suggests that Catholic elementary schools may be relatively better in the wealthier states.

importance on their children receiving a church-related education. Both Vatican II and the decline in the church attendance underlie "age" having a significant positive impact on school enrollment in Dugan's regression. Younger parents are more likely to be responsive to the church's new teachings and their church attendance has declined even more than their elders'.

The decline in individual's demand for Catholic schooling explains only part of the recent turnaround in aggregate demand. As the following data show, enrollment rates for Catholic elementary schools have fallen since 1959:

Year	Enrollment Rate	Year	Enrollment Rate
1955	0.530	1965	0.444
1957	0.531	1967	0.396
1959	0.535	1969	0.338
1961	0.511	1971	0.287
1963	0.486	1973	0.261

(Source: see Table 2-7)

However, throughout most of the 1960s this decline was more than offset by an increase in the number of Catholic school age children (see Table 2-7). Now even that population is declining and hence increasing the decline in aggregate demand. Moreover, that decline is likely to continue due to the recent drop in the birth rate among Catholics, which was even greater than the decline for the nation as a whole.[39]

Many of these factors causing a reduced demand for Catholic education are also having an effect on the other groups of nonpublic schools who have suffered enrollment declines. The decline in participation in organized religion and movement to the suburbs, where competition from the public schools is stronger, is not merely a Catholic phenomenon. In Illinois, for example, many Lutheran schools located in the central cities have had to close their doors as their clientele moved to scattered suburbs.[40] Pressure for increased salaries, which are even lower in Lutheran and Mennonite schools than in Catholic schools,[41] has led to increased tuitions and hence decreased enrollments. Among most other nonpublic schools, costs have risen at a much lower rate,[42] and in most cases demand has been able to keep pace—either because incomes have risen sufficiently or demand is sufficiently inelastic. Among the nonaffiliated schools, problems of relative quality and decreasing participation in organized religion do not exist. Where declines have occurred, as in military academies and single-sex boarding schools, the principal cause seems to be changes in parental and/or student preferences for lifestyle rather than the educational merits of these schools.

Projections

Extrapolating the foregoing evidence to predict what will happen to the equilibrium enrollment in the nonpublic sector in the future is not a safe exercise. On the supply side costs will most certainly continue to rise. The numbers of people entering religious orders is declining rapidly—it has been projected that by 1980 there will be only one-fourth the number of religious teachers there were in 1970[43]—and Catholic and other religiously affiliated schools will have to rely more and more on lay teachers. Moreover, there is no reason not to expect that these teachers will continue to seek parity with their public school counterparts. Second, as Catholic parents perceive public schools to be more substitutable for Catholic schools, these low-spending schools will be forced to improve the quality of their educational programs. Finally, if demand should decline and the schools continue their policy of not consolidating classes, the smaller class sizes will cause per pupil costs to increase.

Such cost increases will likely be translated into decreases in supply through school closings if not by tuition increases. Growth in other sources of private funds—church subsidies and private gifts and endowments—are not likely to keep pace with increases in costs. Church revenues are expected to grow only slightly in the next decade,[44] and with nearly 60 percent of these funds already earmarked for the schools, it is unlikely that further subsidies will be forthcoming. New government aid would seem the only means for averting such a decrease in supply.

A study done for the President's Commission on School Finance estimated that per pupil costs would rise to $851 in Catholic elementary schools and $1,169 in Catholic secondary schools by 1975, if schools are kept open. If schools were fully consolidated so as to maintain current school and class sizes, these amounts would be $500 and $912 respectively.[45]

These increases imply that, in the absence of government subsidy or new source of private funds, tuitions would have to rise by at least $180 or 200 percent, in elementary schools; the comparable figure for Catholic secondary schools is $300, or 88 percent higher.[46] The magnitude of the impact such increases would have on enrollments is not clear. While it is not valid to extrapolate our evidence on the elasticity of demand to these levels, economic theory suggests that, if anything, it should increase. Hence such tuition increases might be expected to cause considerable reductions in nonpublic school enrollments—reductions which would certainly dominate any changes in the remainder of the nonpublic school sector.

What will happen to individual demand is less clear. While it may be likely, it is not necessary that past trends continue. Much of the decline was due to a change in tastes, a reduction in the role of formal religion, and an increasing concern for quality. The people who have continued to enroll their children in the Catholic schools are likely the "hard core," those for whom religion is most important, and hence this source of decline may have run its course.[u] Moreover, some parents have become increasingly dissatisfied with the increasing secularization of the public schools and are turning to the private sector.[47] If the perceived quality of the public schools should worsen from bureaucratization or from increased racial and class conflicts, parents may turn to the nonpublic schools as many have already done in the central cities.[v] If the Supreme Court should uphold a Rodriguez-type case (see Chapter 1), this might spur an exodus from the public schools in wealthy communities.

That changes in tastes and/or living patterns will cause demand to rise sufficiently to offset cost increases is unlikely; for, even if tastes and living patterns remained unchanged, aggregate demand will decline substantially. The number of Catholic school-age children will be 15 percent lower in 1978 than now; and the pool of all school-age children will be 6 percent lower.[48] These changes would imply a reduction of one-half million students in Catholic schools and 80,000 in other nonpublic schools.

Hence enrollments in the nonpublic sector are likely to decline substantially during the 1970s. Supply will be shifting substantially leftward, and given the decline in the school-age population, it is unlikely that individual demand will increase sufficiently to offset this. More likely, it will compound the decline, as suburbanization and the decline of organized religion continue. Estimates prepared for the President's Commission on School Finance suggest that total nonpublic enrollment will decline 2.4 million students, or 54 percent, by 1980:[49]

Type of School	1970	1975	1980
Catholic Elementary	3,359,311	2,150,500	1,407,900
Catholic Secondary	1,008,463	822,245	690,100
Other Nonpublic	914,793	845,300	763,900
Total	5,282,567	3,818,045	2,861,900

If Catholic schools do not consolidate at all, in the absence of large tuition increases they will face an operating deficit of $1,667 million by 1975 and $3,174 million by 1980.[50] Full consolidation would still leave these schools with deficits of $752 million and $1,257 million respectively.[51] In considering the expected decline both in enrollments and in the number of schools, the nation must ask whether the government should aid these schools in reducing this deficit; and if so, whether there are in fact policies that will help, either in stabilizing enrollments or in keeping schools open.

[u]This same argument is frequently made to explain why demand for Catholic secondary schooling has been considerably more stable in recent years.

[v]Note that, barring a large program of public assistance, expansion would have to come in the low-cost part of the sector as not many families can afford the high-cost private schools.

Appendix 2A:
Estimation of the Price
Elasticity of Demand for
Catholic Schools

A simple model of demand and supply and data on prices and enrollments in two periods for each of nearly 800 Catholic schools were used to estimate demand curves for elementary and secondary schools by means of linear regression analysis. A point elasticity for each of the two types of schools was then estimated at average tuition levels.

The basic model used was the following:

$$Q_{i,t}^d = a + bC_{i,t} + cL_iA_t + dL_iP_{i,t} \tag{2A.1}$$

$$Q_{i,t}^s = f(C_{i,t}, K_{i,t}, I_{i,t}/P_{i,t}) \tag{2A.2}$$

$$P_{i,t} = g(K_{i,t}, CC_{i,t}, I_{i,t}) \tag{2A.3}$$

$$Q_{i,t}^d = Q_{i,t}^s \tag{2A.4}$$

where $Q_{i,t}^{d(s)}$ = quantity of enrollment demanded (supplied) for the ith school in period t.

$C_{i,t}$ = Catholic population of the ith school's attendance area in period t.

L_i = location of the ith school.

A_t = certain ascriptive factors in period t (included here are income, education and church attendance; these factors, which affect tastes, are assumed to depend solely on time and changes are treated as constant across schools).

$P_{i,t}$ = price of the ith school in period t.

$K_{i,t}$ = costs of the ith school in period t.

$I_{i,t}$ = a measure of institutional constraints on the ith school in period t.

$CC_{i,t}$ = church collections of the ith school in period t.

The quantity demanded is seen as depending on the Catholic population, a set of ascriptive factors (education, income, and church attendance) of that population, and the price of the school—note that this is consistent with the equations (2.1) through (2.5) in Chapter 2. Supply, on the other hand, is seen as a nearly binary decision: given price, and depending on the Catholic population, costs and certain institutional constraints, should the school be operated? (Actually, the choice could be made to close certain grades.) If it

41

42

is operated, then supply is perfectly elastic with respect to price, up to the school's capacity. Price, in turn, is only partially related to costs, depending also on church collections and institutional constraints. That is, a price is set with only partial regard to market factors, then the school (if operated) offers all its seats at that price and consumer demand then determines equilibrium enrollment. By controlling for changes in the other factors affecting demand, it is believed that our observations on changes in equilibrium price and enrollments represent movements along, or a tracing out of, the demand curve.

Data were collected by the National Catholic Educational Association during the fall the 1972 on a representative sample of 1000 of its members schools (NCEA Standard School Survey Form 1972). Of the returned survey forms (returns = 100 percent), about 200 had to be discarded either because they were incomplete or because they were consolidated during the past year.[a] From the remaining forms, the following data were collected:

1. Level—elementary, secondary
2. Type—parochial, interparochial, diocesan, private
3. Region—Northeast, South, Midwest, West
4. Location—inner city, other central city, suburb, small city, rural
5. Enrollment
   . Tuition and required fees
7. Parish subsidies

Data were collected for both the 1971-72 and 1972-73 school years. While this is a later period than that of the other data in this chapter, it is believed that the elasticity of demand has changed very little.

Returning to the model, to derive a price elasticity, changes in enrollments and prices were considered:

$$Q_{i,t}^d - Q_{i,t-1}^d = (a + bC_{i,t} + cL_iA_t + dL_iP_{i,t}) - (a + bC_{i,t-1}$$
$$+ cL_iA_{t-1} + dL_iP_{i,t-1}) \qquad (2A.5)$$

or

$$Q_{i,t}^d - Q_{i,t-1}^d = b(C_{i,t} - C_{i,t-1}) + cL_i(A_t - A_{t-1}) + dL_i(P_{i,t} - P_{i,t-1})$$

The change in Catholic population in the one year was assumed to be

---

[a]The item most often omitted was information on tuition, fees and subsidies for 1972-1973. NCEA officials advised me that this was generally the result of insufficient accounting capability on the part of the schools and not likely to bias results.

negligible—so that this term drops out.[b] The term $A_t - A_{t-1}$ is treated as a constant. Let

$$DQ_i = Q^d_{i,t} - Q^d_{i,t-1}$$

and

$$DP_i = P_{i,t} - P_{i,t-1};$$

the equation to be estimated then becomes

$$DQ_i = L_i + L_i DP_i + e \qquad (2A.6)$$

DQ_i was taken as the change in total enrollment in each school from 1971-72 to 1972-73. For DP_i, two measures were used: (1) the change in per pupil tuition and fees from 1971-72 to 1972-73; and (2) the change in per pupil tuition, fees and parish subsidies from 1971-72 to 1972-73—this latter measure reflects the belief of many that parents of the church school children actually pay all of these subsidies in lieu of tuition (see Chapter 2). The mean and standard deviation of these variables were:

	Elementary		Secondary	
	Mean	Std. Dev.	Mean	Std. Dev.
DQ_i	−18.6	35.5	−16.1	70.8
$DP_i(1)$	18.1	74.3	31.3	49.1
$DP_i(2)$	30.6	125.5	42.9	73.4

For L_i, an index was developed to combine the effects of both region and type of location—this alternative was chosen because using twenty dummy variables (four regions times five types) left many cells with too few schools. Regressions were run separately using dummies first for the four regions and then for the five types of location. The coefficients on these dummies were then combined[c] and an index value between 1 and 10 was given to each of the twenty locations. The regressions yielded the following results:

A-1 (elementary): $DQ_i = -4.68\ L_i\ -0.021\ L_i DP_i(1),\ R^2 = 0.26$
$\qquad\qquad\qquad\quad$ (0.36)$\quad$ (0.008)

$\qquad\qquad\qquad DQ_i = -4.39\ L_i\ -0.019\ L_i DP_i(2),\ R^2 = 0.27$
$\qquad\qquad\qquad\quad$ (0.36)$\quad$ (.004)

---

[b]This assumption is consistent with data reported at the diocesan level in *The Official Catholic Directory,* 1971 and 1972. Note that this may introduce some error at the parish level. That error is assumed to be random.

[c]Whether the individual effects of the two classes of location were added or multiplied together made virtually no difference on the index values. Note also that of the nine dummies, 7 had coefficients significant at the 5 percent level and 2 at the 10 percent level.

A-2 (secondary): $DQ_i = -2.40\ L_i\ -0.031\ L_iDP_i(1),\ R^2 = 0.05$
                              (1.86)   (0.021)

$DQ_i = -1.22\ L_i\ -0.057\ L_iDP_i(2),\ R^2 = 0.08$
                  (1.84)   (0.026)

While the coefficients of determination are low, the price coefficients in the respective equations are highly significant. Elasticities were then calculated for the following average enrollment and price levels (median values in our sample):

	Elementary	Secondary
Enrollment	280	450
Tuition	$140	$350
Tuition plus Subsidy	$270	$450

Calculating, then

$$\frac{DQ}{Q} \bigg/ \frac{DP}{P}$$

yielded the following results (L_i was factored out—it had an average value of 3.75 for elementary schools and 3.50 for secondary schools):

	Elementary	Secondary
Tuition	−0.04	−0.09
Tuition plus Subsidy	−0.07	−0.19

3

The Economics of a Mixed Supply

For a nation of farmers and mechanics, bent on self government and possessed of the ballot, there was only one kind of educational program in keeping with self-respect, namely a free and open public school system supported by taxation and non-sectarian in its control.

Charles and Mary Beard
(*The Rise of American Civilization*)

The present pattern of government involvement in education evolved during the nineteenth century. As the United States began to expand away from the Atlantic sea coast, the laissez faire notion, "that government governs best which governs least," began to give way to the idea of a more community-oriented government which takes an active role in the promotion of the general welfare—a view which was "nearer to the soil, representing the experience of repeated generations in the establishment of new communities, new territories, and new states,"[1] One product of the large amount of social legislation which grew out of this theory of government in the early nineteenth century was the provision of public funds for education. A large number of child labor laws were passed, restricting parental choice and allowing the community to act in behalf of children; along with these labor laws came compulsory school attendance laws.[2] The leading force in getting both types of laws passed was organized labor—to a large extent acting in its own interest.[3] While funds were forthcoming from all levels of government by the mid- and late-nineteenth century, control of the schools was always maintained at the local level.[4]

The leading economists of this period were largely in accord with these policies. In the tradition of Adam Smith, they believed that the state should take a role in the provision of education,[5] particularly education for the "common people" who were not likely to have the resources nor the inclination to educate themselves.[6] However, like Smith they believed that that role should be a limited one—Smith suggested that state subsidies should be limited to the provision of school buildings and some sort of "voucher" for the poor[7]—and that the schools should be largely voluntary and supported by tuitions.[8] Even John Stuart Mill, who doubted that the market would work very well because parents lacked the necessary information to make good choices, ultimately came to the position that the state should simply require attendance and provide for public inspection and testing;[9] and that "an education established and controlled by the State should only exist, if it exists at all, as one among many competing experiments, carried on for the purpose of examples and stimulus to keep the others up to a certain standard of excellence."[10] But, as noted in Chapter 1, society failed to heed this advice.

Little has changed since the nineteenth century in the way our nation's schools are organized and financed. This chapter will seek to determine under what conditions, if any, these arrangements make sense—and whether modern welfare economics can offer new insights beyond those of the classical economists. The chapter first provides a brief discussion of the nature of the good we call "schooling." Then it explores the difficulties in creating a "market" for education, why a competitive market might fail, and how one might patch up such a market.

Nature of the Good

As Chapter 1 indicated, schooling is many things to many people. Agreement about benefits is very general in nature, and there is no consensus about detailed measures of success. Similarly, in an economic typology, schooling is a very diverse and varied item. Viewed from the production side, perhaps the first point which should be made is that schooling "produces" a service and not a commodity.[11] As such, measurement of output becomes a very difficult task, particularly if one tries to incorporate some notion of quality into that measurement.[12] Such measurement is further complicated by the fact that, unlike commodities, the consumer (parent/student) plays an integral role in the production of the service; to the extent that this input varies considerably, output varies considerably.[13]

A related difficulty is the point, mentioned in Chapter 1, that use of the economic paradigm leads economists to focus on end-products or outputs and ignore the process of producing this service—indeed, economists have in fact tended to consider seriously only a relatively narrow range of outputs. This narrow focus has persisted despite the fact that much of the current criticism of education focuses on the *process* of production. Given the varying role of the consumer in producing educational outputs, this narrowness is a serious weakness. In the absence of a theory of learning, we are very limited in trying to answer such production questions as are there economies of scale, and/or are the various outputs produced jointly or separately?[14]

Discussions aimed at describing the benefits of schooling generally develop two separate divisions: consumption-investment and public-private. With respect to the first dichotomy, economists today are likely to emphasize education as investment: schools produce human capital. The debate has centered on whether this capital is largley cognitive or affective.[a] The recent development of this concept of human capital was viewed as a great advance in the economics of education. The consequences, however, have been mixed. The new research did point out the relation between education and income and that many of the benefits of schooling are enjoyed throughout one's lifetime. But many outputs of schooling that produce more immediate benefits are ignored altogether.[b] Moreover, a lot of energy has been spent in trying to draw what are very arbitrary distinctions. Education produces many outputs which do not nearly fit this typology.[15]

There has also been considerable debate as to what part of schooling generates public benefits and what part private benefits—or, as the debate is often phrased, are there public benefits to education?[16] Generally, economists believe that benefits increasing a person's income or personal well-being should be counted as private benefits.[c] As Chapter 1 indicated, however, education also allegedly provides a number of public benefits: reduction in crime, improved efficiency of the democratic process, and increased economic growth, among others. Critics of such analysis often argue that since we are unable to measure these benefits, we can not be sure they exist, at least not in any substantial amount.[17] Again, it should be noted that many of the distinctions are arbitrary; outputs do not neatly fall into one of these two categories. What should be emphasized is that education is a mixed good; for purposes of forming policy, the key question is to what extent and in what ways can both public and private interests be brought to bear on the provision of education.

In the context of conventional economic theory, this indeterminancy between the public and private nature of the benefits of schooling makes it difficult to determine aggregate demand. As economic theory tells us, to

[a]That is, whether a student's economic productivity is increased because he or she acquired various mental skills, or because he or she is socialized into proper work habits and values. Orthodox economists traditionally have treated it as the former, using verbal achievement tests as a measure of school output. More recently, Herb Gintis has elaborated the latter model and shown that it better fits available data (for citations, see Chapter 1, notes 38 and 62).

[b]For example, schools in effect provide "day-care" services for students—this may be particularly important in the primary grades. Similarly, organized recreation programs are in large part a transfer of leisure activity from the home to the school. Indeed, large expenditures for physical plant in wealthy school districts may generate more consumption than investment benefits.

[c]Note that schooling may affect a person's own income and that of others because it alters the relative supply of various kinds of labor—i.e., educated and uneducated. These benefits or disbenefits are merely pecuniary (i.e., transfers) and should not be counted as real benefits of schooling. It should also be noted, however, that the existence of such benefits implies that a person may be concerned not only with the absolute amount of schooling he or she receives, but with the relative amount (see pages 000-000).

obtain total demand for a mixed good, you vertically sum the individual demands for the private benefits and horizontally sum the individual demands for the private benefits.[18] This problem is further complicated by the interdependency of the utility separate individuals derive from education. To some extent, the benefits I derive depend on there being other educated persons with whom to interact. Hence part of my demand is not for an absolute amount of schooling, but for a relative amount.[19] Similarly, it is the relative amount of education received by various persons which may be important for the output of schooling we have termed "equal opportunity;" that is, the amount of this benefit produced is a function not only of the mean amount of schooling provided, but also of the variance about that mean.

Creating a Market for Education

Economists generally believe that the most efficient allocaters of resources are competitive markets—characterized by consumer sovereignty and choice on the demand side and by a regime of supply where school managers have an incentive to try to attract that demand. To work well, however, a number of conditions need be true: the product is homogeneous; buyers and sellers possess complete information; preferences are exogenous and independent; and producers have well-specified production and objective functions. To a greater or less degree, all of these conditions may be violated in the case of schooling. The possible outputs of schooling, as we have shown, are not even well-specified, let alone homogeneous. Schools with the same apparent inputs may produce a very different quantity or mix of outputs. This situation would make it very difficult for buyers (parents) to make well-informed choices.[20] The search for the necessary information can be characterized as "intensive" rather than "extensive,"[21] with the result that the market may be a high-cost means of providing that information.[22] Moreover, people's preferences for schooling are not exogenous—if only because of the existence of compulsory attendance laws and the powerful role in most communities at the local school board[23]—and to the extent that schools produce public benefits, individual preferences are not independent.

Similarly, the necessary conditions for producers may not be met. Information is limited; and the absence of a good theory of learning noted earlier (see Chapter 1) makes it difficult, if not impossible, to specify a production function. This difficulty is further added to by the fact, noted earlier, that the consumer plays an integral role in the production of education. In a sense this means that our choice of how to produce education is not limited to the public sector or the private market, but may also include nonmarket intrafamily production.[24] This may be precisely the choice parents of Catholic school children make: to place their children in a very low expenditure school and to increase their own input into the production of their child's education.[d] Even if we had knowledge of how the various outputs of schooling are produced, it is not clear that the schools are well-designed to, in some sense, "efficiently" produce those outputs or to respond to changes in demand. Schools are highly decentralized and nonhierarchical—individual teachers have a large amount of independence and control—making the industrial, unique production function model to some extent irrelevant.[25] Moreover, the incentive structures of school managers, as well as teachers, are not closely tied to satisfying demand.[e] Finally, even if it were useful to use such a model, it may be that there are scale economies in the production of schooling which would make the market a less useful method of organizing production.[26]

For a number of reasons, then, a competitive market may "fail" to produce an efficient or optimal outcome. Even if not—that is, even if none of these "distorting" factors are present—we may want to interfere with or to place a number of constraints on the workings of such a market. Education may, to some extent, be classified as a "merit want"—part of its output demanded by the community as a group rather than as a collection of individuals.[27] The argument of this type most often made is the argument for "protection of minors": the community has an obligation to protect the welfare of its young, and hence a right to interfere with the possible preferences of the children's parents.[28] At a minimum, this argument has led most Western societies to impose compulsory school attendance laws.[f]

We may also think of the two supposed outputs of schooling, equal opportunity and the instilling of a common set of values, as merit wants. Both of these desired outputs might lead to more active government interference with the market. The issue here might be put in terms of "how standardized a product do we want."[29] In the case of equal opportunity, the issue is one of standardizing the amount of education received—making the choice of how much education you receive not dependent on your ability to pay. For the instilling of common values, the issue is standardizing the

[d]If a greater proportion of parental input represents the utilization of previously unused resources (i.e., parents' time), or if parents get positive satisfaction out of this activity, then Catholic instruction has lower real costs than public instruction. Otherwise, greater parental input represents a shift from cash outlay to "payment-in-kind."

[e]This point is discussed in more detail in Chapter 4, together with the related point that there is little incentive to attract demand because "successful" firms can not expand to capture a larger share of the market.

[f]Note that given labor's role in passing these laws, it is possible to interpret them as protecting working men and women against the competition of docile children in the labor market. Schools do more than provide instruction; they also keep kids out of work and under efficient supervision.

quality or type of education received. These issues lead us to ask what constraints should be placed on which participants. Do we constrain the parents' freedom to choose, either on the grounds that they often have their own interest, rather than their children's, in mind, or on the grounds that some parents are more competent to choose than others and to allow freedom of choice would be to preserve the existing inequities?[30] Or, do we constrain the producers—school administrators and/or teachers—on the grounds that they might attempt to instill values in students which run counter to the interests of the large part of the community? The answer as to which participants to constrain depends largely on our having better knowledge of how parents make choices and how the outputs of schooling are in fact produced. The answer to how extensively we constrain the market depends largely on philosophical and ideological issues.[g] Once these issues are settled, the question becomes whether these outputs of schooling are better produced in a well-planned or publicly produced system, or through a largely competitive or private market system.[h]

The earlier discussion of possible "market failures" considered reasons why the government might want to intervene in the allocation of resources to education—that is, on the demand side of the market. While such failures provide a rationale for partial or complete government financing of schools, they offer no rationale at all for the government becoming involved in the production of schooling. Only consideration of the desirable constraints implied by the presence of what we have termed "merit wants" can provide such a rationale.[31] I do not mean to imply that public production is ill founded. It may in fact be that the rationale for the public production of schooling is much stronger today than the rationale for public subsidy of schooling.[i] However, it is important in considering public-policy choices to keep these two issues separate. The presence of public benefits from schooling does not imply public production. In fact, it may not even imply public subsidy.[j] The relevant consideration for subsidy is not whether positive public benefits are present, but whether they are present *at the*

[g]Note that the choice is not between total market freedom and total constraint. The government could establish a system of regulation to impose any degree of constraint it thought necessary.

[h]The debate appears to center around the nature of the limited information possessed by buyers and sellers. If the problem is in having the technical knowledge of how the outputs of schooling can best be generated, or which outputs (e.g., reading ability) will best satisfy ultimate student "needs" (e.g., a better job), then it is argued that education specialists (e.g., school administrators) should have more say—and implicitly that central planning would be more efficient. This is particularly true if there are externalities which a publicly planned system could internalize. If, however, school officials lack information as to what the ultimate "needs" of their clientele are, then some use of the market to elicit this information would seem in order.

[i]Note that we could have a system of public production together with user charges in place of tax revenues.

[j]I want to thank Robert Hartman for help in clarifying the following points.

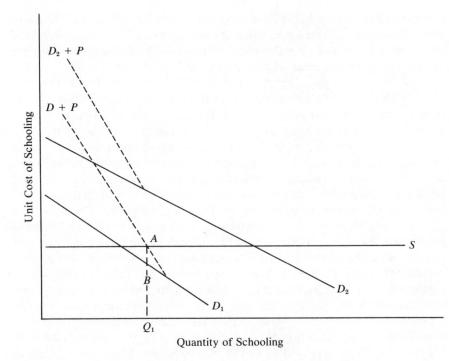

Figure 3-1. Declining Marginal Public Benefits to Schooling and the Optimal Subsidy

margin. If declining marginal public benefits are associated with increasing amounts of schooling, this may not be the case. In Figure 3-1 above, D_1 and D_2 represent two individuals' private demand for schooling, S represents the common supply curve, and P represents the marginal public benefits at each level of output (drawn as an addition to demand). As the diagram shows, while public benefits are present in both cases, only in the case of D_1 should there be public subsidy, and then only in the amount AB per unit for Q_1 units—the community will receive the remaining public benefits anyway and to subsidize them will not increase the public benefits derived from schooling, but rather the consumer surplus of the individual receiving the subsidy.[32]

The existence, then of certain market failures, of public benefits to schooling, or of merit wants may all serve to limit the private market's usefulness in allocating education resources. One might then ask what is a second-best solution to the provision and/or production of schooling,[k] or what set of conditions will make the current system desirable from an economist's viewpoint? Under a system of competitive production, a

---

[k]Or, what is the optimal amount of government intervention? Note that the market may still be the low cost alternative.

generalized subsidy scheme to achieve the optimality condition (shown in note 18) would yield an equal per-unit subsidy to each of the s persons of αC_q, where ($0 \leq \alpha \leq 1$) is the share of total demand represented by the second term of each equated pair, and would yield a market price of $(1 - \alpha)C_q$, with each of the s persons consuming the amount implied by this price.[33] The share of total output which is subsidized depends then on the relative importance of public as opposed to private benefits.[l] While all individuals receive an equal subsidy per unit, the share of their purchases which is subsidized also depends on their own personal valuation of public versus private benefits.[34] If we believe that many of the public benefits of q actually are "social" wants, we might simply introduce society as the $s + 1$ person, a person who does not consume q himself or herself, but who gains satisfaction from q being consumed by the other s persons. To each of the equated pairs, then, we could add the term V_a^{s+1}. If society views all citizens alike, then the share of public benefits in each equated pair is increased equally with the optimal subsidy continuing to be uniform across all s persons. If, however, society is concerned with who is consuming q—say, it gains benefits from improving the relative equality of consumption—then the presence of such a term now may imply a different amount of subsidy for each of the s persons. The subsidy is also affected if the value of public benefits becomes relatively less important as output is increased (as in Figure 3-1). Then there will be an output above which the second term in each equated pair equals zero—and the optimality conditions will be essentially the same as for a private good. This point might be reached either because individuals highly value the private benefits or because the marginal cost of q is very low.

As noted in Chapter 1, the present system of schooling in this country is not competitive, but is dominated by a system of "pure communal provision" at the local level.[m] Under a system of communal provision an optimal overall subsidy scheme would involve charging each person a price equal to his or her marginal valuation of the uniform output and subsidizing the balance.[n] In addition, however, the existing system also has a nonpublic element, although these nonpublic schools are a small part of the overall

---

[l]Whether the outputs are consumption or investment does not affect this partial analysis in itself—assuming that future benefits are property evaluated, i.e., measured as present values.

[m]The first-order condition for optimal provision under an equal-consumption constraint of communal provision is

$$[V_a^1 + \sum_{i=1}^{s} V_b^i] + [V_a^2 + \sum_{i=1}^{s} V_b^i] + \ldots + [V_a^s + \sum_{i=1}^{s} V_b^i] = sC_q$$

Note that the amount by which this constraint reduces optimal benefits without the constraint depends on the degree of homogeneity of the population. If all s persons are identical, there is no reduction in benefits at all.

[n]Note that, as in the market case, the total subsidy is equal to the share of total demand at the margin which is public.

system. An optimal subsidy scheme in this case where there is communally provided public schooling together with the option of choosing a nonpublic school would be similar to the case where just public school is available. Note, however, that the subsidies for public and private schooling need not be identical.[o]

In fact, our method of financing schools is very different from this subsidy scheme. The subsidy to public schools, in most cases, is essentially total—the price a family pays is in effect equal to the marginal cost of providing the communal amount of schooling to one more student times $1/r$, where $1/r$ is the family's share of the district's tax bill (i.e., if the family enrolls its child in the public school, costs in that school increase by some amount, of which the family pays $1/r$. The subsidy to the private school is determined by the budgetary process. In the case where only public schooling exists, this subsidy scheme may be efficient if the s persons' private tastes are relatively similar, if there is a voting mechanism which chooses the optimal amount,[35] and a positive social value is placed on equalizing consumption.[36] It may, though, distort the relative pricing (and hence relative consumption) of public and nonpublic schooling—assuming that the budgeted subsidy for nonpublic schooling covers only a fraction of the schools' costs.[p]

Despite the virtually total subsidy of public schooling, in a regime of communal provision it may be rational for some persons to choose nonpublic schooling. First, many nonpublic schools are largely operated by various religious groups and are not necessarily perfect substitutes for publicly produced schooling. That is, while it frequently may appear that people are paying a positive sum for a service they can receive free, it may in fact be that they are purchasing a service not provided by the public schools, namely religious instruction.[q] Parents may also be concerned with whom their children attend school and be willing to pay for a select set of classmates.[r] Finally, some parents may simply desire a substantial amount more of some educational services that are communally provided. Given that schooling is a very "lumpy" good, the choice of private education may be entirely rational.

Conceptually, all three of these sources of demand for nonpublic schooling are identical: individual parents have sufficiently higher demand

[o]Note that allowing choice in the quantity of schooling increases benefits, but all of this increase is in private benefits.

[p]Note that this subsidy includes both aid to parents, via some form of a voucher scheme or tax credit, as well as aid to the schools themselves.

[q]See Chapter 2, note p. This analysis is also applicable to other types of nonpublic schools, such as military academies or schools which offer special programs not found in the public schools.

[r]This is a problem principally in large districts. To a large extent, parents select classmates for their children by residing in the type of school district (i.e., community) they want.

for one or more of the outputs of schooling than the amounts communally provided and so make the switch from public to nonpublic schooling.[s] As Figure 3-2 shows, this choice depends not only on the level of demand of the particular output, but on the real cost (to the individual) of available private schooling.[37] In the diagram, D_m represents the demand for schooling of the median family in the community—taken as the level of public schooling provided[38]—D_i the demand of the ith individual, and OP the real cost of a unit of public schooling (assumed to be constant over the relevant range). In the case of the individual who simply demands a higher level of similar outputs than the local public system provides, the person will choose nonpublic schooling if the ABC area is greater than the $OPAQ_m$ area.[t] If D_i represents parents who want a select set of classmates for their children, they presumably perceive such a change as increasing productivity (reducing the real unit cost) of their children's schooling.[u] Assume such a change would lower the unit cost to OP'. Then these parents will opt for nonpublic schooling of $A'BC'$, which is a greater area than $OP'A'Q_m$. In the case of the parent who wants religious instruction, D_i might be interpreted as follows: the ith such parent has the same demand for the outputs of public schooling as the median family in the community, but it also has a demand for religious instruction[v] so that the gap between D_m and D_i represents the demand for an output of schooling which is not produced in the public system. In this case, the parent will choose nonpublic schooling if the area $ARSC$ is greater than $OPAQ_m$. Moreover, if the school is partially subsidized by the church[w] so that cost to the parent is less than total cost, say OP', then the parent will choose church schooling of the area $A'ARSC'$ is greater than $OP'A'Q$.

For a number of reasons, it may be socially desirable to subsidize nonpublic schooling at a lower level than public schooling. Returning to our model (Figure 3-2), in the first case, D_i must be substantially larger than D_m, and the resulting Q_i substantially larger than Q_m. If there are diminishing returns to the public benefits of schooling and the public system is being

[s]While parents can in part privately supplement their child's public education with tutors, music lessons, dance lessons, and so forth, the choice is primarily a binary one: public or private school.

[t]This ignores the tax saving from the public schools having to educate one less child. For the individual, this saving is assumed to be negligible.

[u]This is consistent with accepted theory that a student's classmates are an important input to his or her schooling. It should also be noted that these students, in leaving the public system, may raise costs in that system (costs for which they do not pay). Some have argued that this is a real problem today in large central cities (see Chapter 4).

[v]It is assumed that religious instruction could be jointly produced with no appreciable change in the unit cost of schooling.

[w]Religious instruction may generate public benefits to a subset of the community, so that they in part subsidize it. More active involvement of parents, discussed earlier, may also cause total unit costs to fall. The analysis is similar in both cases.

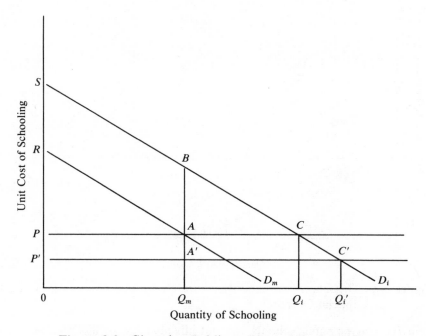

Figure 3-2. Choosing Public or Nonpublic Schooling

optimally or near-optimally subsidized, then this i^{th} family should not be subsidized for sending its children to nonpublic school (see Figure 3-1). The result is similar to the ith family choosing a different set of classmates for its children. While the level of the demand curve for such a family may actually be below that of the median family in the community—if OP' is sufficiently less than OP—the quantity of schooling Q_i it chooses must always be greater than Q_m quantity of schooling.[x] Thus it is likely that it would be inefficient to subsidize these families to send their children to nonpublic schools. In the case of the family seeking religious instruction, however, it may actually choose a quantity of schooling which is less than that publicly supplied. As Figure 3-3 shows, if the demand of the ith such family for the outputs of schooling is sufficiently below that of the median family in the community, or if it is only somewhat below the median family and its demand for religious instruction—drawn as an add-on to demand for other outputs—is highly inelastic, then Q_i may be less than Q_m. In this case, there may be grounds for partially subsidizing such schooling of this family. Moreover, in all three cases, there are intramarginal families for whom some level of subsidy would cause them to make the switch to nonpublic schools. If the nonpublic schools, though, are producing fewer public

---

[x]This is the only way for ABC to be positive. How low the individual's demand may be and still induce him or her to switch depends on how relatively important an input the child's classmates are in its education.

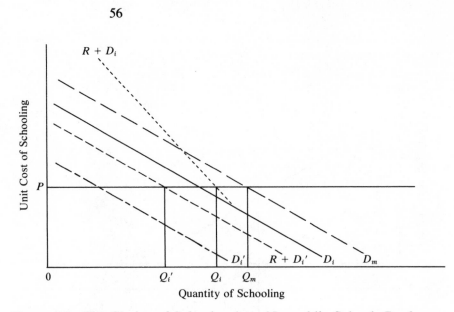

Figure 3-3. The Choice of Schools where Nonpublic Schools Produce a
Special Output

benefits than the public schools, the unit subsidy must always be lower than
the level of subsidy in the public school. Moreover, if aid cannot be targeted
to these intramarginal families, then the unit level of subsidy must be
sufficiently below the public school level so that total aid divided by the
intramarginal families is less than the unit subsidy in the public schools.[y]

This analysis implies that public and nonpublic schooling are similar in
producing public benefits. This in fact may not be the case. If society is
concerned with placing constraints on the production of schooling
—implying the presence of social or merit wants—it may in fact evaluate
public and nonpublic schooling differently. The result may be a discontinuity in the stream of benefits between the two types of schools, irrespec-
tive of the relative levels of output, and hence a discontinuity in the prices
may be desirable. Absence of a complete voucher scheme provides that
discontinuity.[39] If society views regulation of the private sector as an
alternative to public production, then this discontinuity of benefits may
disappear within the constrained range. Such regulation is likely to be more
feasible in the case of constraining the quantity of schooling—reflecting
society's concern for equal opportunity—than in the case of constraining
the type of instruction—reflecting society's concern for instilling a com-

[y]Note that even if marginal benefits are positive, they may be offset by negative pecuniary
externalities. If Di is reflecting a demand for religious instruction, it would be necessary to
show why children cannot go to public school and get religious instruction after school.(See
note 40.) And if parents are seeking to reduce costs by putting ''good'' students together, they
are by the same token raising costs in the classrooms from which the ''good'' students are
removed (see note u).

mon set of values in its youth. A similar discontinuity may arise if the nonpublic school jointly produces an output that produces zero benefits for a portion of society if it is unsubsidized, but produces substantial disbenefits if it is subsidized. This would appear to be the case with church schools providing religious instruction. Public subsidies for religious instruction generate substantial disutility for many members of the community.[z] At issue, at least theoretically, is whether church schools are really an educational alternative to the public schools where religious doctrine also happens to be taught, or are they in fact an integral part of the religious mission of the respective churches.[aa] Put in a policy context, do these schools perform purely secular activities that can be identified as distinct and independent from their religious activity?[40]

In the absence of social wants, it may still be desirable to provide a smaller unit subsidy, for a given level of output, to the nonpublic school than to the public school. It may be that the mix of outputs in the nonpublic school is more weighted to private benefits or that the nonpublic school is "less efficient" at producing public benefits. Both cases imply that public benefits of the public schools are greater at the margin than public benefits of the nonpublic schools for the same level of output. On the other side, however, if we accept schooling as a heterogeneous, or potentially heterogeneous, good and consumers as possessing heterogeneous tastes, we may also view the nonpublic school as generating an output called "choice," to which all persons attach a positive value, even if they do not exercise that choice.[41] This implies that, other things equal, the public benefits in nonpublic schools will be larger than those in public schools and hence for a similar output, a larger subsidy would be warranted. Similarly, the nonpublic schools, in providing competition and diversity to the public schools, presumably increase the productivity of education generally, that is, both public and private. Since such increases imply an increased consumption of both public and nonpublic schooling, and hence a lowering of the public subsidy otherwise required, society may want to in part subsidize the production of diversity.

The preceding analysis on whether to subsidize various types of non-

---

[z]Many see this as a violation of the principle of separation of church and state, an important freedom in this country. The disutility it causes is evidenced by the active and costly legal battles many groups, such as PEARL and POAU, wage in court and in state and federal legislatures to block such subsidies.

[aa]That religious instruction is a joint product is true, at least with regard to the Catholic schools. The National Conference of Catholic Bishops has recently stated that in Catholic schools,

students are instructed in human knowledge and skills, valued indeed for their own worth but seen simultaneously as deriving their most profound significance from God's plan for His creation. Here, too, instruction in religious truth and values is an integral part of the school program. It is not one more subject alongside the rest, but instead it is perceived and functions as the underlying reality in which the student's experiences of learning and living achieve their coherence and their deepest meaning.

public schools implicitly assumes that the benefits to the public from a child's secular schooling are independent of whether that child attends a public or nonpublic school. In fact, this may not be the case. If one of the principal public benefits is socialization of children, a freely run private system may hinder social solidarity. However, limited dissent is often viewed in this country as having a positive value, so that a small private sector might actually increase public benefits.[bb] Another case is the situation noted earlier where a family opts for the nonpublic school to achieve a select set of classmates. In this case, the unit cost of nonpublic school may fall and that of the public school rise comparably.[cc] This would imply a relative increase in the consumption of nonpublic schooling, and hence a relative decrease in the unit subsidy of nonpublic schooling. Moreover, if nonpublic schooling generates less public benefits per unit than public schooling, this shift will represent a decrease in the total public benefits from schooling—whether it represents an increase or decline in total schooling depends on the relative demand elasticities of public and nonpublic schoolgoers.

Finally, there is the situation discussed earlier where the parents of students attending the nonpublic school choose a more active role in their children's education. If their time is otherwise unutilized, then the unit cost of the private school will fall, without the public school's cost rising. Or, we may view the change from the benefit side: productivity is increased so that at the same unit cost, the value of all the outputs are increased. In either case, the relative consumption of the private school will be higher, and hence the unit subsidy, other things equal, will be lower. But society benefits from this increased productivity and hence its willingness to subsidize it may offset the decline from increased output.[dd]

In addition to possible public benefits of the nonpublic schools, within the present institutional framework the choice to directly subsidize the nonpublic sector must take account of a constrained government budget. With a constrained budget, in choosing between two groups of recipients—for example, public and nonpublic school children—the group

---

[bb]As with equal opportunity, it may be that achieving the illusion of choice and diversity in the system generates many of the same benefits (except possibly the improvement of quality of instruction) as achieving real choice and diversity. In this case, a very limited nonpublic sector can generate benefits, without generating the costs of a highly diverse system. Note that a very small nonpublic sector could generate a substantial amount of innovation. Also note that a small sector could generate many of the benefits of choice if most people never chose to exercise that choice.

[cc]If there are diseconomies in the homogeneous grouping of students, as is the conventional wisdom, then total average cost will rise—i.e., public school costs will rise more than proportionately. If the nonpublic school is small, relative to the public school, this increase will be small. However, it must be counted as a negative public output of the nonpublic school. The results here are the same as if the public system operated on a segregated basis.

[dd]Here there is room for bargaining—see note 34.

with the more elastic demand, other things equal, should receive the larger share of funds.[42] Similarly, one must look at only whether a given program generates positive public benefits, but whether it generates greater benefits than some alternative social program.[43] Finally, given that education produces a whole vector of outputs and that we lack a good learning theory for any of them, policymakers must take account of the impact of different government subsidy and regulatory programs on the type of output produced.

Nonpublic Schools and the Public Sector

In light of current constitutional and fiscal matters, it is the Panel's considered judgement that public interest requires the Federal Government to take major initiatives toward a solution of the financial crisis in nonpublic education.

President's Panel on Nonpublic
Education *(Final Report)*

As pointed out in Chapters 1 and 2, much of the current debate over aid to nonpublic schools has focused on the rapidly rising costs, and accompanying enrollment declines, in existing nonpublic schools. It is the expected gap between costs and revenues in these schools that the President's Panel has termed a "crisis," asserting that parents of nonpublic school students cannot afford the burden of additional tuition to meet the expected increases in cost. As pointed out previously, by 1975 Catholic schools alone are forecast to have an operating deficit of $1.67 billion. Much of the rest of the sector is similarly operating in the red. For example, over half of the NAIS schools have reported that expenses exceeded income for each of the last three years.[1] In Chapter 3 we saw that two types of policy instruments are available to the government, if it wished to help offset that deficit: some form of voucher to the individual student (or parent) and/or some type of subsidy to the schools themselves.

This chapter examines the arguments that have been put forward both in support of and opposed to the position of the President's Panel. It does so in the context of a mixed system of supply and focuses primarily on the current policy discussion surrounding aid to the existing nonpublic schools and/or their students. The arguments are examined in light of the theoretical discussion in Chapter 3 and in light of what empirical evidence there is to support or refute these arguments. As noted in Chapter 2, there are actually two dimensions to the policies being espoused: (1) public aid to maintain enrollments in the existing nonpublic schools; and (2) public aid to keep the existing nonpublic schools fiscally solvent and operating. Three types of arguments have been advanced in behalf of these policies: economic, social, and educational. While there is some overlap, the economic arguments have been used principally in support of the first dimension of the policies, while the social and educational arguments have largely been employed in support of the second dimension. Those opposing all aid have relied on a combination of economic and social arguments, together with a strong case that such aid may be unconstitutional. Because of the peculiar relation of these legal issues to the present analysis, they are dealt with separately in this chapter's Appendix 4A.

The Economic Arguments

The Nixon administration and its two school commissions seem primarily concerned with aid to maintain nonpublic school enrollments. The principal argument on which they rely for asserting that "the public interest requires" such aid is a fiscal one. By attending nonpublic schools, these students save the taxpayers money; if they should decide to transfer en masse to the public system, a tremendous new burden would be placed on the public treasury. Moreover, given that nonpublic students, as detailed in Chapter 2, are concentrated in a few states and in large central cities, the burden would be disproportionately heavy on these jurisdictions, many of which are already fiscally strained. The president has asserted, "If the nonpublic schools were ever permitted to go under in the major cities in America, many public schools might very well go under with them, because they simply couldn't undertake the burden."[2]

For the individual student (or family), the schooling choice is virtually a binary one: to accept the type and amount of schooling that is communally provided, or to choose an alternative type and/or amount offered by one or more nearby nonpublic schools.[a] As shown in Chapter 3, the individual will make the switch if the net additional benefits of private schooling exceed the cost to the individual. Some given increase in the costs of nonpublic schooling, then, will cause some individuals to switch back (note that this will happen even if costs rise comparably in the public school since, under communal provision, the individual's cost burden is independent of whether his or her children do or do not go to the public school). Moreover, if nonpublic schools close, students may simply be forced to make the switch.

The choice facing the government, however, rests solely on the *public* benefits generated by the two types of schools. If the government is indifferent between public benefits being generated at a public or nonpublic school, then the criterion for subsidy is whether it is less expensive, in terms of additional costs to the government, to subsidize students in the nonpublic schools and/or to subsidize the schools themselves, or to simply absorb students into the public schools?

[a]This ignores the possibility of moving to another nearby public school district. See discussion below.

The total costs of absorbing students into the public system were estimated for the 1972-73 school year by first estimating the "excess capacity" in the public schools in 1972-73, and then, second, for all students to be absorbed beyond this capacity, estimating an average marginal cost of absorbing them.[3] That is, it was believed that in many instances public schools are operating below capacity and that a certain number of students could be absorbed in many areas with virtually no increase in costs.[4] Beyond this capacity, new students would impose additional costs close to current average per pupil costs. Certainly the marginal cost of absorbing nonpublic students is likely to be more continuous, increasing from zero to near average per pupil cost as more and more students are added. However, since many expenditure decisions are very "lumpy," this two-step approach was viewed as a good first approximation.

Capacity of the public schools was determined by multiplying the highest enrollment figure among the 1970-71, 1971-72, and 1972-73 school years by the ratio of the highest pupil/teacher ratio in those three years to the pupil/teacher ratio in the year with the peak enrollment. The assumption here is that if large numbers of students are to be absorbed into the public system, many will be "squeezed in" in the form of larger class sizes—in part filling empty seats created by the recent decline in the number of public school children. It is further assumed that recent history (i.e., the past two years) is a good estimate both of what is feasible and what is likely to be acceptable to the local community. This approach also assumes that the traditional method of one teacher-one classroom is still the method overwhelmingly employed—that is, such changes as schools without walls or team-teaching have a negligible impact on the calculations. "Excess capacity" was taken as the difference between "capacity" and actual 1971-72 enrollments. The average marginal cost of absorbing students was estimated in two steps: first, teacher costs were estimated by multiplying the number of additional teachers needed by the average annual salary of teachers;[b] secondly, this number was increased by a percentage equal to the fraction that nonteacher variable costs were of teacher costs—capital costs were treated separately (see below). Included in "variable costs" were other instructional expenditures and expenditures for administration, transportation, health, plant maintenance, and other student services. Excluded were plant operation and fixed charges—it is assumed that these costs are incurred regardless of the number of students in the school. The result was that marginal cost in the short run over this limited range typically equalled about 80 percent of average per pupil cost.

[b]This method probably provides an upper bound on teacher costs, for two reasons. First, the estimate of the number of new teachers required may be high since it does not take into account the expected decline in public school enrollments after 1972-73. Secondly, the salary figures may be high since new teachers are likely to be paid less than the average salary of existing teachers because new teachers necessarily have less seniority.

Ideally, these calculations should all be made at the local level. Unfortunately, data for such a calculation are largely unavailable. As a first approximation, therefore, state-by-state data were used. Calculations based on such data implicitly assume that nonpublic school students within a given state are located in the same areas as the excess capacity in that state's public schools. To the extent that they are not, the costs of absorption must be increased. Some evidence may be gleaned from Swartz's study, which estimated excess capacity by type of region within states.[5] On this basis, he found that excess capacity is concentrated in central cities and their suburbs, where in fact most nonpublic schools are located.[c] The sources of the various data used, and the actual calculations are contained in this chapter's Appendix 4B.

Considerable variation across the fifty states was found in all three components of the calculations. "Excess capacity" ranged from zero to as much as 10 percent, the average being about 2 percent.[d] As noted in Chapter 2, nonpublic enrollments varied from 2 percent to 20 percent of a state's total enrollment. Finally, the average marginal cost of absorbing excess nonpublic students ranged from a low of $485 per pupil to a high of $1050 per pupil. In the aggregate, the results of these calculations find that for 1972-73, absorbing all nonpublic school students into public systems would have increased current expenditures in those systems by about $2.9 billion.[e] This is an increase of about 5 percent over present levels. Even in New York State, which would be the hardest hit, current expenditures would rise by only 15 percent.

Capital expenditures may represent an additional source of increase in costs. The increase in these costs is much harder to estimate, for two reasons: first, only a fraction of these costs are attributable to any one budget year; and, secondly, the public system may be able to purchase, at a much lower cost, vacant nonpublic school buildings; this has been frequently done in the past. If it is assumed that no nonpublic school buildings are purchased, and that we can attribute to all nonpublic students above "excess capacity"—as defined earlier, an amount equal to the average per pupil capital cost of a new school within each state[f]—then absorption of all nonpublic students in 1972-73 would have meant an additional public expenditure of 6 billion in construction costs.[g] If these buildings were

---

[c]Because of possible mobility within metropolitan areas, the usefulness of a more localized analysis is limited. See below, pp. 122-24.

[d]It should be noted that changes in pupil/teacher ratios had no effect on estimated capacity in thirty-one states and only a very slight impact in the remaining states.

[e]This amounts to nearly $600 per nonpublic school pupil—including those who presumably could be absorbed at near zero cost.

[f]This probably gives us an upper bound on construction costs, since much new construction is likely to be in the less expensive form of additions to existing schools.

[g]Data sources and calculations are in Appendix 4B.

financed through bond sales, this would represent an additional annual expenditure of $400 million, or only 0.8 percent of total annual public school expenditures.[6]

Total collapse of the nonpublic sector, however, is not a likely outcome in the foreseeable future, even in the absence of additional public aid.[h] A more reasonable estimate is that the present rate of enrollment decline might increase to 20 percent. In 1972-73, this would have resulted in the public schools absorbing an additional 450,000 students[i]—essentially all from the Catholic schools. Using the same methodology as in estimating the cost of total collapse, it is estimated that absorbing these students would have increased public school current expenditures by some $190 million.[j] This represents an increase of only 0.4 percent—for New York, again the highest state, the figure is 1.1 percent.

The above figures hardly represent the disaster so often depicted by advocates of aid to nonpublic schools. These aggregate figures, however, mask what may be a very severe impact for certain areas and localities. Many large central cities, which have as many as 50 percent of their students enrolled in nonpublic schools, are already running large deficits. A study done on Philadelphia, for example, showed that if all Catholic schools had closed, the city's public school system would have had to increase expenditures in 1972-73 by $147.5 million,[7] or 40 percent over the actual 1972-73 budget. If the rate of decline had simply doubled, this would have necessitated $7.5 million in additional public school expenditures[8]—given Philadelphia's projected 1972-73 deficit of $30 million, this is not a small amount. There are two factors, however, which tend to reduce the local impact of nonpublic school transfers. The first is that not all public school costs are borne by the local community; a large share comes out of the state treasury—the average is about 45 percent in states with large nonpublic school enrollments. What share of the marginal costs the state would bear depends on the particular nature of the state formula.[9] The second factor is the potential residential mobility of nonpublic school families. The evidence suggests, for example, that when students drop out of Catholic schools in central cities—where over half of all Catholic students are enrolled—their families tend to move to the various surrounding suburbs, rather than enroll in the central city's public schools.[10]

[h]Such a collapse would imply that every nonpublic school family was at, or near, the margin. In fact, the high inelasticity of aggregate demand for nonpublic schooling suggests this is not the case.

[i]The rates of decline in the respective states were increased proportionately and then added together. Increasing the rate of decline to 20 percent meant increasing each states actual rate of decline by a factor of 2.4.

[j]This amounts to an expenditure of over $400 per pupil absorbed—this is less than the $600 per pupil expenditure to absorb all students because excess capacity plays a relatively larger role. Also, it is assumed here that there would be no construction costs, at least in the short run, and that all transferring students would fit into existing classrooms.

The potential costs of absorbing nonpublic school pupils into the public system must be compared, then, with the public subsidies that would be necessary to keep these students in their present schools—that is, to keep schools from closing and to keep students in other nonpublic schools from transferring. One policy might be to subsidize the nonpublic schools sufficiently to hold costs to families constant—that is, to cover the operating deficits.[k] In 1972-73, this policy would have implied a subsidy of over $1 billion.[11] While this is far less than the cost of absorbing all nonpublic school students into the public schools, it is more than four times as costly as absorbing the additional 450,000 students who represent the far more likely possibility of increasing the rate of transfer to 20 percent. An alternative policy is to consider what impact a $190 million subsidy—the cost of absorption—would have on nonpublic enrollments. If the money could be targeted completely on those students who are about to transfer or on the schools about to close, it would mean a per pupil subsidy of over $400. In terms of the choice implied by Figure 3-2, only persons with substantial changes in taste are likely to be unswayed by such a large subsidy.[l] However, at least at the federal level, there is no conceivable subsidy program which could so target its funds. Aid must be shared, to some extent, with students not intending to transfer and with schools not about to close.[m] Were it shared equally, the per pupil subsidy would be only $40, an amount likely to influence only a fraction of the students intending to transfer.[n] In a few states, however, where excess capacity in the public schools is low and the number of likely transfers is a high fraction of nonpublic enrollment, a state-financed subsidy program might have some impact even if fully shared by all nonpublic school students. In Michigan, New York, Ohio, and Pennsylvania, a subsidy program equal to the absorption cost implied by increasing the present rate of transfer to 20 percent would yield a per pupil subsidy of about $100. Moreover, locally financed programs would allow even further concentration on potential transferees.

There is an additional reason for local or state, rather than federal, financing of such a subsidy program—if in fact it is felt that this argument is sufficient justification for such subsidies. The taxpayers in the states and

---

[k]Such a policy is consistent with the general thrust of the argument as it is made by aid advocates.

[l]See Chapter 3. Note that, as presented, changes in taste and comparable changes in cost are equivalent.

[m]While it would seem to be easier to target funds if they were given directly to the schools, note that the autonomy of individual nonpublic schools, even those affiliated with the same church, makes sharing of aid funds—i.e., shifting private funds to schools in trouble as public monies become generally available—very unlikely. Moreover, aid to schools is less likely to gain political support—or to be found constitutional—than is aid to students.

[n]If our estimate of the elasticity of demand for nonpublic schooling is representative, the subsidy, viewed as an avoided increase in tuition, would reduce the number of transfers by only 30 percent.

localities where nonpublic schools are concentrated are precisely those taxpayers for whom these schools purportedly save money. The taxpayers of New York City and New York State are better off because nearly one-half million of the city's children attend nonpublic school. A federally subsidized program would involve large transfers from the taxpayers of states with low nonpublic enrollments to those in states with high such enrollments. Utah, for example, with 98 percent of its students in public schools, would receive virtually no benefits from such a program, but would help to subsidize the taxpayers of Rhode Island—who now enjoy a large tax subsidy from the parents of nonpublic school students—where nearly 20 percent of all students are in nonpublic schools.

In sum, for a number of reasons it is not at all clear that keeping nonpublic schools operating and keeping students in them will save tax-payers money. First, there is some excess capacity in the public schools —and as enrollments continue to fall over the next few years, more will be created. Secondly, many students are transferring not because of price increases or school closings, but simply because they no longer want a sectarian education. Finally, the immediate total collapse of all nonpublic schools simply is not very likely; and unless aid can be targeted on those students who are about to transfer, its impact will be diluted.

The second economic argument made in behalf of aid to nonpublic school students or their families is an equity argument, that these families bear a double burden in supporting their children's education; they pay taxes for the local public schools—which entitles them to enroll their children there—and they pay tuition to the nonpublic schools. By sending their children to nonpublic schools, they reduce the tax burden of the rest of the community. In a sense, this argument might be viewed as the other side of the same coin from the previous argument; nonpublic school students save the taxpayers money precisely because the families of these students bear a double burden. However, this argument is concerned with the equity rather than efficiency aspects of government subsidies. Moreover, it actu-ally focuses on an issue which the previous argument assumed away, the discontinuity in the prices of public and private schooling—that is, society is not necessarily indifferent to whether a child is educated in a public or private school.

The argument here is not merely that families are paying for a public service from which they receive no direct benefits. All tax-supported programs are financed in part by persons who do not directly benefit—and to opt for a complete system of user charges is to deny that there are any indirect, or spillover, benefits from these tax-supported programs. Nor is the argument that a family should be reimbursed for simply abstaining from a public service for which it is eligible as, say, in the case of the family choosing to use private recreational facilities rather than add to the conges-tion of those facilities that are publicly supported; for while the family's non-use of the public facilities does produce a social benefit in lower congestion, its private consumption of recreation itself generates no public benefits. However, in the context of compulsory school attendance laws and state regulation of nonpublic schools, it is argued that opting out of the public system implies similar consumption, and similar consumption externalities, in the private sector.

As was pointed out in Chapter 3, this may not be the case. The relative shares of public and private schooling which are optimally subsidized may differ not only because one is producing at a higher level—and hence the marginal public benefits are lower—but may differ even at equal levels of production because of the presence of social, or merit, wants which are evaluated differently for the two types of schools. As was pointed out, however, the public gets a "free ride" on all public benefits that are intramarginal. And, as Mark Pauly has demonstrated, there is room for efficient bargaining between the government and families of nonpublic school students (see Chapter 3, note 34). The double-burden argument is an effort to establish just such bargaining—on grounds of fairness. It should be noted that this argument does not necessarily imply that the public aid should be total, only that it should be greater than zero[o]—or, in the current policy context, greater than subsidies currently received. In the absence of the above bargaining, advocates of increased aid must show that additional aid will generate more additional public benefits than costs. Moreover, in the context of a constrained government budget, they must show that these benefits are larger than those generated by an alternative government expenditure of the same amount—for example, an expenditure to absorb nonpublic school students into the public schools.

A concern for equity is also one of the principal arguments used by opponents of public aid for nonpublic schools. They argue that such aid would represent a perverse redistribution of income—funds would flow from the general population into the hands of wealthier families. Although data on the respective economic backgrounds of public and nonpublic students are sketchy, Table 4-1 shows that, at least on a national basis, nonpublic school students do indeed come from wealthier families. Much of this difference in the family income of public and nonpublic school students, however, may be a consequence of nonpublic schools being concentrated in areas, particularly the urban North and East, where family incomes run above the national average. Few studies have been done comparing the family incomes of public and nonpublic students within a local area. There have been, however, two recent studies comparing the incomes of Catholic school families with the entire local population. A study of New York City, which contains 10 percent of the nation's nonpub-

---

[o]If, for example, public benefits in nonpublic school equalled zero, the aid should be the family's tax burden times 1/the number of students in public school—i.e., the effective price of public schooling.

Table 4-1

Percentage Distribution of Public and Nonpublic Elementary and Secondary School Students, by Family Income Class, Fall 1972

	Elementary		Secondary	
Family Income	Public	Nonpublic	Public	Nonpublic
Under $3,000	8.2	1.8	5.9	1.7
$3,000-4,999	13.0	5.0	9.6	4.6
5,000-7,499	16.9	8.4	14.9	5.8
7,500-7,499	16.1	14.7	14.9	13.0
10,000-14,999	27.3	38.3	30.1	27.3
15,000 and Over	18.5	31.8	24.6	47.6
Total	100.0	100.0	100.0	100.0

Source: U.S. Bureau of the Census, *Current Population Reports,* Series P-20, no. 260 (February 1974), Table 13, p. 46. Data do not include kindergarten enrollment.

lic schools, found that while the median income for Catholic school families was slightly below the median for the city as a whole, fewer than 2 percent of Catholic school students came from welfare families, less than one-tenth the proportion of public school students who did.[12] Similarly, a study of the Archdiocese of St. Louis found the following results:[13]

	Median income of Catholic School Families	Median Income of All Families
St. Louis City	$ 8,752	$ 8,182
St. Louis County	12,040	12,392
Outlying Areas	9,282	9,509

Other nonpublic schools in these regions, most of which have much higher tuitions than the Catholic schools, presumably enroll wealthier students. It must be noted that Catholic school families in these studies are compared to the general population. In 1972, overall median family income was $11,116.[14] As Table 4-1 shows, while public secondary school families have a similar median, more than 60 percent of public elementary school families have incomes below this figure. This difference raises the question of what group is the appropriate standard of reference for considering redistribution implications: taxpayers (i.e., the general population) or alternative beneficiaries (i.e., public school families.) Objections to aid based on the redistribution could easily be overcome by targeting aid via a means-tested program, like Title I. However, given that few low-income families are enrolled in nonpublic schools, such a program would have little impact on either total enrollments or the number of schools operating. A program that used the poverty income level of $4,200 as a ceiling would reach only

200,000 students currently enrolled, or 4 percent of the nonpublic total. To have a real impact, the program would have to generate substantial numbers of transfers from public to nonpublic schools.

The Social and Educational Arguments

There are two other major arguments made in behalf of aid to nonpublic schools, one "social" and the other "educational." In an economic typology, both are arguments that there exist externalities peculiar to nonpublic schools, externalities which may override the simple cost comparisons sketched above. The first of these arguments is that nonpublic schools in central cities generate public benefits in two ways. These schools keep middle-class white families in the central cities, thus improving the city's tax base and helping to maintain stable integrated neighborhoods. President Nixon has argued:

For many Americans, allegiance to their nonpublic community schools is their strongest and sometimes, perhaps, their only single tie to city life. If their schools should close, many of these families would abandon the city and go to the suburbs. This, in turn, would further worsen the social isolation of our central cities—a development we must not permit.[15]

In addition, these schools are alleged to provide an educational alternative for inner-city minorities; Mr. Nixon has called them, "beacons of hope . . . continuing the effort to maintain good schools in these poor and racially isolated communities."[16] In the context of Chapter 3, nonpublic schools are seen to generate social benefits not generated by the public schools. Hence, other things equal, the optimal subsidy to these schools should be increased.

There is strong evidence that the presence of nonpublic schools has greatly helped to keep many white families in the large central cities, thus enlarging the cities' racial and socioeconomic diversity. As Table 4-2 shows, within central cities, nonpublic schools have a considerably higher percentage of white enrollment than do the public schools.[p] Many of these nonpublic schools, particularly Catholic ones, are located in the cities' ethnic neighborhoods, helping to some extent to maintain such enclaves. Moreover, as Wilbur Cohen points out in his study of Chicago, Detroit, Milwaukee, and Philadelphia, when nonpublic schools close in the central city, the families affected frequently move to the suburbs.[17] That nonpublic schools are a key factor in maintaining stable integrated neighborhoods, however, is much less clear. First of all, very few such neighborhoods

---

[p]Moreover, in cities such as Washington and New York, for example, these include most of the children of wealthy families, who without such schools would likely move to the suburbs.

Table 4-2

Percentage of School Children Attending Public and Nonpublic Elementary and Secondary Schools, by Race, Selected Cities, 1970

City	Black and Spanish-Surnamed		White and Others[a]	
	Public	Nonpublic	Public	Nonpublic
New York	88	12	55	45
Washington	93	7	48	52
Boston	93	7	64	36
Philadelphia	91	9	43	55
Newark	95	5	66	34
Detroit	95	5	64	36
Cleveland	96	4	69	31
Chicago	91	9	57	43

[a]"Other" includes Orientals and American Indians, but these constitute a miniscule fraction of the total.

Source: U.S. Bureau of the Census, *1970 Census of Population: General Economic and Social Characteristics,* PC(1), volumes for the respective states, Tables 83, 91, and 97 in each volume.

exist. As Table 4-3 shows, most large central cities, at least those with significant nonpublic enrollments, have highly segregated housing patterns. Data from the Cohen study on Detroit and Chicago and data from a separate study on New York City, indicate that nonpublic schools do enroll a significant fraction of the students in these integrated neighborhoods. However, they represent a minute fraction of the cities' total enrollment or of total nonpublic enrollment. Moreover, many other neighborhoods that were integrated have become highly segregated despite the presence of nonpublic schools.

That nonpublic schools provide an educational alternative for inner-city minorities is also not clear. As Table 4-2 showed, most nonpublic schools enroll few minority students' let alone disadvantaged minority students. Data from the Catholic schools, which comprise by far the bulk of nonpublic inner-city schools, indicate that no more than 3 percent of Catholic schools serve a predominantly disadvantaged clientele in city poverty areas, and low-income minority students probably make up no more than 3 percent of Catholic enrollments.[18] Other nonpublic schools have been established in the ghettos in recent years, and some expensive private schools have increased their scholarship programs; but added together, a best estimate is that about 1 percent of inner-city minority children attend nonpublic schools.

Most people would agree that the improvement of racial and socioeconomic integration and the improvement of educational opportunities for inner-city minority children represent positive social benefits.

Table 4-3
Racial Segregation in Housing Patterns for Selected Cities, 1960 and 1970

City	Taeuber Index of Segregation, 1960[a]	Percentage of Census Tracts Integrated, 1970[b]
New York	79.3	16.0
Philadelphia	87.1	
Chicago	92.6	4.3
Los Angeles	81.8	4.2
Detroit	84.5	11.3
Pittsburgh	84.6	6.0
Boston	83.9	8.5
Milwaukee	88.1	5.8

[a]Index based on city block data from the 1960 U.S. Census. A score of zero indicates complete absence of segregation; a score of 100 means complete segregation. Source: Karl E. Taeuber and Alma F. Taeuber, *Negroes in Cities: Residential Segregation and Neighborhood hange* (Chicago: Aldine Publishing Company, 1965), Table 1, p. 32.
[b]"Integrated" menas the presence of at least 30 percent of both whites and blacks. Source: U.S. Bureau of the Census, *1970 Census of Population and Housing: Census Track Reports,* Series PHC(1), Table 2, volumes for the respective metropolitan areas.

Moreover, from a redistributive viewpoint, strengthening the tax base of central cities at the expense of its suburbs is generally viewed as a net social gain. However, it is far from clear that aid to nonpublic schools is society's optimal means of generating these benefits. For nonpublic school families to improve the cities' fiscal position, they must contribute more to the treasury than they receive in form of subsidies. This is likely to happen only if an aid program can be targeted on those likely to leave, not an easy task. Moreover, it must be asked whether a similar subsidy to the public schools, or even the provision of some other social services, would not have a larger impact. Similarly, subsidies designed to provide better educational opportunities for inner-city minorities must be compared with other programs, for example increasing funds for Title I or ESEA—given the small size of the nonpublic school sector in the inner city, aid designed to produce a major expansion of this sector would seem necessary if it is to be an efficient mechanism for achieving the above aims.[q] Finally, even if aid to nonpublic schools is found to be efficient, it is not clear that it would be socially desirable. At a time when the principal institution society has chosen to use for fostering integration is the schools, aid designed to maintain segregated schools for the sake of more integrated housing patterns would seem to be counterproductive.

[q]As Chapter 3 pointed out, the mere illusion of choice may produce some public benefits. Otherwise, if the sector is not expanded, society is faced with the tradeoff of giving a lot to a few students through nonpublic school subsidies, or something to a large number of students through subsidies to the public schools.

Table 4-4

Number of Different Public School Districts in Selected Metropolitan Areas, 1970

Metropolitan Area	Number of School Districts
New York	192
Boston	77
Chicago	325
Philadelphia	218
Pittsburgh	134
St. Louis	108
Detroit	97
Los Angeles-Long Beach	83
San Francisco-Oakland	83
Portland	85
Kansas City	105

Source: Seymour Sacks, Ralph Andrew with Tom Carnevale, "School State Aid and the System of Finance: Central City, Suburban, and Rural Dimensions of Revenue Sharing" (Syracuse University, no date; processed), Table I.

The second "externality" argument for public aid is that these schools offer an alternative to the public system, and that education is of such importance that people ought to have a choice. Moreover, the nonpublic schools are a source of diversity and competition, helping to keep the public schools on their toes and improving the general quality of elementary and secondary education. Mr. Nixon has emphasized this point in his message to Congress and in his speeches, asserting that it would be intolerable for a "single school system" to "ever gain absolute monopoly over the education of our children."[19]

As pointed out in Chapter 3, choice may be viewed as one of the public-benefit outputs of schooling, implying that other things equal, the production of choice should warrant a higher public subsidy. Implicit in the argument made by Mr. Nixon and other advocates of aid is that nonpublic schools are the only source of choice open to the community and that they in fact do offer a substantial alternative. Neither of these assumptions may be accurate. Within most metropolitan areas, where nonpublic schools are concentrated, families have a large number of school districts from which to choose (see Table 4-4). If Tiebout's theory is operative, those systems will offer a variety of education possibilities for those families both willing and able to move about the area. For families who are not, [r] however, the nonpublic school may be the only alternative to the local public school. Even so, the choice it provides may in fact be very limited. Given that 80

[r]Many families may be unable to freely move about the metropolitan area because of economic limitations or racial discrimination.

percent of existing nonpublic schools are Catholic and incorporate Catholic doctrine as an integral part of all classes, many parents may see this as no choice at all. Moreover, given that members of the local Catholic community are given first access to these schools,[s] if demand for them were increased, non-Catholic families might still be left with no choice. The few nonsectarian schools which do exist generally charge high tuitions, hence making them an alternative only for the wealthy in the absence of substantial public assistance.

That these schools offer a substantial educational alternative is also doubtful. For example, the Fleischman Commission study of New York State concluded, "by and large, public and nonpublic schools are very similar with respect to methods of teaching and the substance of what is taught."[20] The need for variation and diversity is clear. As the study by Averch et al. showed, no single variant of school technology has been found to be the best in all situations. The choice these schools provide, however, is much more whether the teaching of religious values will take place in the school or through some other means and what sort of classmates a student will have. Both of these choices generate more private than public benefits.[t]

Similarly, as Chapter 3 indicated, real competition and diversity are viewed as generating social benefits by increasing the productivity of schooling. Implicit in arguing for aid to nonpublic schools on this basis is the assumption that market forces will generate educational innovations. There are many problems with such an assumption. Although many volumes have been written on the subject of innovation in education, about all that can be said with certainty is that education seems very resistant to other than surface change.[21]

Various writers have suggested a number of theories of the innovation process and reasons why market forces may not be particularly effective in generating innovations. As Richard Nelson has pointed out, [22] innovation depends not only on supply side factors, but also on the consumers' demand for innovation. Given the limited information possessed by parents and/or the desirability of explicitly interfering with their consumer sovereignty, pressure from consumers may be very weak.

A related difficulty is in defining what constitutes an innovation. If we limit the concept to changes which increase productivity or output, we are faced with the problem of defining what the schools' output is supposed to be. Given that different communities, or different school boards, may have

---

[s]Such preferences seems reasonable, given that a large share of schools' operations are subsidized by the church. Moreover, many state laws have been written so as to make this form of discrimination legal.

[t]See Chapter 3. Also note that the division these choices represent may generate social disbenefits in weakening social solidarity.

very different "desired outputs," what constitutes an innovation for one school may not for another. Even if outputs were known and well-defined, the problem arises of knowing what inputs affect them. As Matthew Miles points out, "innovations" may involve adding new materials or personnel, introducing new technologies, reorganizing the curriculum, the school's decision-making processes, or the organization of the school, among others.[23] Many of these changes may have only very indirect impact on output. Given the complex nature of the production process in education, and hence the effort that must be expanded to understand how a new procedure or device will impact upon that process, "newness" is often equated with "innovative." If parents or the local community bring pressure on a school to innovate, adoption of something "new" often alleviates that pressure, even if it is misused so as to have no effect.[24]

Even if there is demand for innovation,[25] there are a number of factors on the supply side hindering their adoption. School boards and school administrators are generally satisficers rather than maximizers[26]—given their limited information, it is difficult to be much else— and hence search for innovations is very limited. Moreover, schools are decentralized organizations and there are many forces within a school system which act to maintain the status quo.[27] For example, both the formal reward and promotion system, as well as the informal social and psychological "rewards" from peers, encourage teachers and administrators to maintain existing systems and methods.[28]

Moreover, the organization of the education sector tends to slow the diffusion process. Innovative teachers and/or innovative public schools cannot expand to serve a larger share of the market. Since for the most part nonpublic schools are too small a part of the market to seriously challenge the monopoly power of the public school, the "survival space" of these schools is quite substantial.[29] The result is that today researchers have found that outside competitive pressures have had little impact on school systems; the decision to innovate has depended almost solely on the people and conditions within the innovating system.[30]

Given our very limited knowledge about the education process and a constantly changing environment, it would seem that experimentation must be an integral part of any widespread innovative effort.[31] Nonpublic schools, however, are not the only possible source of such experimental efforts. There is tremendous diversity within the public sector. Today there are nearly 17,000 school districts nationwide, ranging in size from fewer than 10 students to more than 1 million students, and in annual expenditures from less than $200 per pupil to more than $14,000 per pupil. It is true that a number of forces tend to make these independent systems behave more like part of a national system.[32] Nonetheless, there is still considerable experimentation going on within the public sector.[33] Moreover, successful innovations arising out of this experimenting are more likely to be diffused because of the tendency of most school officials to adopt new practices or structures from similar systems.[34]

The forces that tend to link public schools together also operate to make nonpublic schools very much like their public counterparts.[35] Moreover, the severe budget limitations of most Catholic and Lutheran schools—they frequently have available to them less than half the resources that neighboring public schools do—leave these schools with little margin for innovative or experimental programs. To be sure, there are a number of innovative and experimental nonpublic schools, but they educate only a small fraction of the total school population. Moreover, it is not clear just how good a model these schools are for public systems. Certainly for many of the different types of innovations listed above, particularly organizational changes, small autonomous schools would not seem to be appropriate guides. For other types of innovations, though, these schools may be the only testing grounds, because of bureaucratic or political or union constraints on the public systems. However, the weak links between the two sectors may hamper diffusion.[36]

If what is sought is for real pluralism and diversity to become a characteristic of America's schools, and if it is believed that competitive forces can help this aim, then more than merely preserving the existing nonpublic schools is necessary. In the absence of substantial reorganization of the public sector along more competitive lines,[u] public aid sufficient to cause a large expansion of the nonpublic sector—to reduce the monopolistic survival space of the public schools—must be forthcoming. For this goal to be desirable, the gains from such pluralism must outweigh possible losses from a weakening of social solidarity.

Opponents of public aid to nonpublic schools also argue that these schools produce a special externality, but they contend it is a negative one. Nonpublic schools increase overall segregation in the schools, and hence hamper the goals of social solidarity and equal opportunity. However, unlike the first argument against aid which alleges that nonpublic schools generate additional social disbenefits only if they are subsidized, this argument suggests that these schools generate disbenefits whether or not they are subsidized. It is clear that nonpublic schools enroll a substantially smaller proportion of minority students than do the public schools. As Table 4-5 shows, the proportion of minorities in nonpublic schools is less than half that of the public schools. In central cities, moreover, the differ-

---

[u]Such a reorganization might be accomplished by a "voucher" system within the public sector, which allows students to choose among local public schools, or among programs with a school, and allocates revenues to schools, or programs, on the basis of these choices. (The Office of Economic Opportunity has funded an experiment along these lines in the Alum Rock Union Elementary School District in San Jose, California, and plans similar experiments in other cities.)

Table 4-5
Ethnic Composition of Public and Nonpublic Schools, Fall 1972 (Percentage)

Type of School	White	Minority[a]
Public		
Elementary	78.8	21.2
Secondary	80.4	19.6
Nonpublic—Catholic		
Elementary	85.7	14.3
Secondary	89.0	11.0
Nonpublic—Non-Catholic		
Elementary	96.3	3.7
Secondary	96.0	4.0

[a]Minority includes blacks, American Indians, Orientals, and Spanish-surnamed Americans.

Sources: U.S. Bureau of the Census, P-20, no. 222, Table 4; and National Catholic Educational Association, *A Report of U.S. Catholic Schools, 1973-74,* p. 13.

ences are even greater (See Table 4-2), with the result that meaningful integration in the public schools is seriously hindered. In many northern areas, however, little effort has been exerted to desegregate the public schools.[37] The marginal effect on integration of an aid program for nonpublic schools in these regions is likely to be minimal. While additional aid may keep more whites in nonpublic schools,[v] previous discussion suggests that in the absence of aid many white families will not transfer their children to the cities' public schools, but will move to the suburbs. Note also that the earlier argument suggests that hampering society's efforts to integrate the schools for the sake of helping to integrate neighborhoods is actually a social benefit. This must be decided by the communities themselves.

In the South, the case is somewhat clearer. Many of the private academies that have been set up to avoid court-ordered integration are on shaky financial grounds. Public aid may be just what these schools need to become viable in the long run.

To the extent that these schools do increase segregation in the schools, they probably do hinder the goal of equal opportunity—this is consistent with the findings of the U.S. Supreme Court since it declared in 1954 that "separate educational facilities are inherently unequal."[38] Moreover, to the extent that nonpublic schools frequently enroll the better qualified students and leave less qualified or "problem" students to the public schools, they further hamper equal opportunity.[w] However, whether these schools hinder the goal of social solidarity is largely a question of values.

[v]Note that such aid might help keep tuitions down or scholarships sufficient to allow minority students to continue to enroll in these schools.

[w]The nonpublic schools are not alone here; the multitude of exclusive suburban school districts have a similar impact.

What some call "devisive," others see as "diversity and choice" that enrich the system.[39] Presumably, government regulation could ensure that what a community views as essential common values are taught in all schools. Aid could be withheld from schools that did not comply. Similarly, aid might be withheld from schools that discriminate. However, given our lack of understanding of how students learn and the subtleties of discrimination, both such constraints may be very difficult to work out in practice.

The integration argument against aid to nonpublic schools and the equity argument discussed earlier both take the form of these schools producing social disbenefits which, other things equal, should reduce the optimal level of public assistance. The final argument against aid is more in the form of a constraint which many feel should be placed on the whole choice. It is argued that since most nonpublic schools are church-related, aid to them represents the establishment of religion and hence violates the First Amendment of the U.S. Constitution. It will be for the courts to decide whether this constraint should prohibit all aid, aid to those schools which are church-subsidized, or certain types of aid. Further discussion of these issues is left to this chapter's Appendix 4A. Excluding a total ban of aid, [x] the foregoing arguments suggest that the case for general subsidies for nonpublic schools and their students is considerably weaker than the case for smaller, targeted aid. The burden of proof for any aid, however, would still seem to be on the proaid advocates.

---

[x]Such a ban is unlikely since it would mean a reversal of recent court decisions, which have allowed limited aid for items such as textbooks and transportation (see Appendix 4A for citation).

Appendix 4A:
The Constitutional Issues in
Aid to Nonpublic Schools

The First Amendment of the U.S. Constitution reads in part, "Congress shall make no law respecting an establishment of religion, or prohibiting the free exercise thereof." Many people believe that this clause prohibits public aid to nonpublic schools because the vast majority of those schools are operated and subsidized by organized religion.[1] There would seem to be two issues involved here. The first, mentioned in earlier chapters and related to the final proaid argument, is whether church-related schools are really an educational alternative to the public schools where the teaching of religion is an additional and independent activity or whether in fact these schools are an integral part of the religious mission of the respective churches. Even if it decided that they are an educational alternative, it must be decided how indirect public aid must be before it does not constitute aid to religion.[a]

The "aid-to-religion" issue will ultimately be decided by the Supreme Court, which has been slowly refining its position on this question in a number of decisions handed down over the past twenty-five years.[2] In 1947 the Court upheld tax-supported transportation for nonpublic school pupils in New Jersey.[3] In so doing, it ruled that while direct aid to nonpublic schools was illegal, the provision of public welfare services must be provided to all, even though they may indirectly aid religion.[4] Sixteen years later the Court outlawed the reading of the Bible in public schools[5] Here it established the principle that for a law not to violate the First Amendment, it must have "a secular purpose and a primary effect that neither advances nor inhibits religion."[6] This test was refined in 1968 in a decision that upheld a New York State law which permits the state to loan secular textbooks to nonpublic school students.[7] Here the Court was careful to point out that the books were loaned to the students and not the schools and also that because there was no proof that the religious and secular activities of the schools were inexorably intertwined, the argument that these secular texts would be used for a religious purpose had little basis. In 1970 the Court upheld the tax-exempt status for church properties on the grounds that such exemptions avoided "excessive government entanglement."[8]

In 1971 the Court pulled together and more clearly defined the criteria on which to determine the constitutionality of public aid to nonpublic schools. In a decision handed down June 28, dealing with three cases

---

[a]That is, at the extreme any aid which benefits a member of a church indirectly benefits the church itself since it leaves the individual with more income, part of which he or she may contribute to that church. The economist might argue that the appropriate distinction is whether the gain to the church is the result of an income effect or a substitution effect.

jointly, the Court ruled that a Pennsylvania law and a Rhode Island law, both granting salary supplements to teachers in nonpublic schools, violated the religion clauses of the First Amendment.[9] The Court was careful to point out that Jefferson's "wall of separation" between church and state was not absolute; certain contacts were found to be "necessary and permissible," among them, "fire inspections, building and zoning regulations, and state requirements under compulsory school attendance laws."[10] As criteria for determining the constitutionality of statutes in this area, the Court developed a threefold test: "First, the statute must have a secular legislative purpose; second, its principal or primary effect must be one that neither advances nor inhibits religion . . . ; finally, the statute must not foster 'an excessive government entanglement with religion,'"[11] Because of the supervision that would be required to ensure that teachers taught secular subjects and not religion, both laws were found to violate the third criteria. The Court went to some length to explain that any statute involving even a minimum of government supervision would probably be found to violate this criteria.

Finally, in June of 1973 the Court put severe limitations on the types of aid which might pass this threefold test by interpreting the second criterion very strictly. [12] The following programs were all found to "advance religion": (1) reimbursement to nonpublic schools for activities, such as the keeping of certain records, which are required by the state; (2) aid for maintenance of nonpublic school buildings; (3) flat grants to parents of nonpublic school children as reimbursement for tuitions already paid; and (4) fixed-amount tax credits for nonpublic school tuitions (credits which the court saw as identical to grants). The Court was careful not to rule out all aid, noting that "some forms of aid may be channelled to the secular [activities of nonpublic schools] without providing direct aid to the sectarian [activities]. But the channel is a narrow one."[13] It is not clear, however, what specific programs are likely to gain approval.

Economists expend a lot of energy arguing that two seemingly different activities or politics are in fact identical. Lawyers, on the other hand, spend much time drawing distinctions between apparently similar activities and policies. For policymakers concerned about the legal aspects of public aid to nonpublic schools, four distinctions appear to be important:[14] (1) Is the *target* of the program both public and nonpublic schools, or only nonpublic schools;[15] (2) is the *objective* of the program to abstain from taxation or to give aid which requires an appropriation; (3) Is the *form* of the aid cash or particular services, facilities, or materials; and (4) Is the *channel* of the aid the parent, the student, the teacher, or the school? Most legal scholars believe that the more indirect the aid, the better its chances of passing judicial muster (see discussion of tax credit proposals in Chapter 5).[16]

To date, all of the legal discussion has focused on the First Amendment.

However, given the recent success of Serrano-type cases, the President's Panel believes that supporters of aid to nonpublic schools may have reason to begin emphasizing the equal protection provisions of the Fourteenth Amendment in their legal arguments.[17] Even should these legal issues be resolved in favor of the nonpublic schools, the economic and social objections will still need to be answered.

Appendix 4B: Estimated Costs of Absorbing Nonpublic School Students into the Public Schools

The costs of absorbing all (and a given fraction of) nonpublic school students into the public schools are estimated for the 1972-73 school year. Current operating expenditures and capital expenditures are treated separately.

Estimated Increases in Current Operating Expenditures

Increases in current operating expenditures were estimated by first determining "excess capacity" within the public schools and then by estimating an average marginal cost of absorbing these nonpublic school students beyond that capacity—for description of the method used, see Chapter 4, pp. 63-64. State by state estimation of excess capacity is found in Table 4B-1. Table 4B-2 contains state by state comparisons of excess capacity with the number of nonpublic school students to be absorbed under the assumptions that (1) all nonpublic school students are to be absorbed, and (2) an increase to 20 percent in the number of transfers from nonpublic to public schools. An estimate of the marginal cost of absorbing excess nonpublic students in each state is found in Table 4B-3. The total increase in current operating expenditures from absorbing all nonpublic students was then obtained by multiplying each entry in column 3 of Table 4B-2 by the corresponding entry in column 5 of Table 4B-3, and then summing over the fifty states. This calculation yielded a total estimated increase in current operating expenditures of $2.9 billion. To estimate the increase in current costs resulting from increasing the rate of transfer to 20 percent, each entry in column (5) of Table 4B-2 was multiplied by the corresponding entry in column (5) of Table 4B-3, and these products were summed. This calculation yielded an estimate of $190 million.

Estimated Increases in Capital Costs

Increases in capital costs were estimated only for the assumption of a total collapse. The estimate was made by multiplying each entry in column (3) of Table 4B-2 by the corresponding entry in either column (2) or column (4) of Table 4B-4. This calculation yielded an estimate of $6 billion.

Table 4B-1

Estimation of Excess Capacity in the Public Schools, 1972-73

State	(1) Peak ADM 1970-71 to 1972-73[a]	(2) P/T Ratio Adjustment[b]	(3) Capacity 1972-73[c]	(4) Actual ADM 1972-73[a]	(5) Excess Capacity 1972-73[d]
Alabama	800,537	1.00	800,537	777,271	23,266
Alaska	84,800	104	88,192	84,800	3,392
Arizona	507,240	1.04	527,530	507,240	20,290
Arkansas	436,815	1.00	436,815	435,289	1,526
California	4,968,000	1.00	4,968,000	4,707,100	260,900
Colorado	573,000	1.01	578,730	573,000	5,730
Connecticut	676,728	1.03	697,030	674,667	22,363
Delaware	133,150	1.00	133,150	132,870	280
Florida	1,472,467	1.04	1,531,366	1,472,467	58,899
Georgia	1,098,780	1.00	1,098,780	1,090,477	8,303
Hawaii	181,473	1.02	185,102	179,000	6,102
Idaho	185,114	1.13	209,179	184,663	24,516
Illinois	2,282,927	1.00	2,282,927	2,282,927	–0–
Indiana	1,172,272	1.00	1,172,272	1,161,390	10,882
Iowa	655,401	1.00	655,401	648,019	7,382
Kansas	488,550	1.00	488,550	471,867	16,683
Kentucky	708,033	1.00	708,033	701,000	7,033
Louisiana	838,460	1.04	871,998	838,460	33,538
Maine	246,750	1.00	246,750	246,750	–0–
Maryland	917,298	1.03	944,817	916,629	28,188
Massachusetts	1,170,000	1.09	2,212,523	1,170,000	105,300
Michigan	2,212,523	1.00	919,000	2,193,738	19,785
Minnesota	919,000	1.00	527,774	912,411	6,589
Mississippi	527,774	1.00	1,078,347	520,320	7,454
Missouri	1,078,347	1.00		1,030,008	48,339
Montana	174,989	1.03	180,239	172,056	8,183

State	(1)	(2)	(3)	(4)	(5)
Nebraska	329,860	1.00	329,860	325,500	4,360
Nevada	130,000	1.04	135,200	130,000	5,200
New Hampshire	164,600	1.00	164,600	164,600	—0—
New Jersey	1,507,900	1.05	1,583,295	1,507,900	75,395
New Mexico	285,022	1.02	290,722	285,022	5,700
New York	3,515,318	1.00	3,515,318	3,515,318	—0—
No. Carolina	1,171,310	1.00	1,171,310	1,139,932	31,378
No. Dakota	146,818	1.00	146,818	141,564	5,254
Ohio	2,405,216	1.00	2,405,216	2,390,836	14,380
Oklahoma	612,466	1.02	624,715	580,300	44,415
Oregon	469,425	1.00	469,425	465,734	3,691
Pennsylvania	2,353,500	1.00	2,353,500	2,345,900	7,600
Rhode Island	189,096	1.01	190,987	187,000	3,987
So. Carolina	628,395	1.03	647,247	620,000	27,247
So. Dakota	166,075	1.00	166,075	160,615	5,460
Tennessee	897,290	1.00	897,290	891,000	6,290
Texas	2,681,250	1.00	2,681,250	2,668,300	12,950
Utah	304,500	1.02	310,590	304,500	6,090
Vermont	109,710	1.01	110,807	109,710	1,097
Virginia	1,067,996	1.00	1,067,996	1,060,128	7,868
Washington	817,712	1.00	817,712	790,502	27,210
West Virginia	412,176	1.00	412,176	412,176	—0—
Wisconsin	953,512	1.00	953,512	952,023	1,489
Wyoming	86,231	1.00	86,231	85,331	900

[a]In five states average daily membership (ADM) was not available. In these cases, fall enrollment was used—the five are Idaho, Michigan, Missouri, Montana, and Washington.

[b]Adjustment calculated as highest pupil-teacher ratio in the three years divided by pupil-teacher ratio in year of peak enrollment.

[c]Capacity calculates as column (1) times column (2).

[d]Excess capacity calculated as column (3) minus column (4).

Sources: enrollments from National Education Association, *Estimates of School Statistics, 1971-72* (NEA Research Report 1971-R13) and *Estimates of School Statistics, 1972-R12* (NEA Research Report 1972-R12)—Tables 2, 3 and 4 in each volume; pupil-teacher ratios were derived from the same two volumes, using Tables 5 and 6 in each volume to obtain numbers of classroom teachers (i.e., pupil-teacher ratio for a given state in a given year equals ADM/total classroom teachers.

Table 4B-2
Estimation of Excess Nonpublic Students, 1972-73, Under Two Assumptions

	(1) Total Catholic Enrollment 1972-73	(2) Estimated Total Other Nonpublic Enrollment 1972-73[a]	(3) Excess Nonpublic Transfers— Assumption I[b]	(4) Number of Nonpublic Transfers 1972-73[c]	(5) Excess Nonpublic Transfers— Assumption II[d]
Alabama	16,988	42,088	36,560	750	—
Alaska	913	386	—0—	—0—	—
Arizona	19,043	9,553	9,911	1,605	—
Arkansas	9,026	3,657	11,080	—0—	—
California	269,515	109,206	124,367	8,468	—
Colorado	20,940	10,100	26,586	1,276	—
Connecticut	71,146	25,005	78,204	5,643	—
Delaware	15,937	2,299	17,131	232	230
Florida	75,952	54,545	73,458	1,960	—
Georgia	14,510	21,007	27,198	100	—
Hawaii	14,759	7,801	15,513	—0—	—
Idaho	2,624	2,078	—0—	124	—
Illinois	353,007	64,778	436,859	19,074	44,200
Indiana	77,664	21,996	93,864	5,086	—
Iowa	57,876	10,240	63,035	2,301	—
Kansas	29,474	3,121	17,012	1,100	—
Kentucky	52,639	5,276	54,215	3,333	720
Louisiana	110,627	29,919	15,853	2,573	—
Maine	9,676	7,976	18,701	1,049	2,416
Maryland	81,207	29,013	86,032	5,105	—
Massachusetts	144,751	30,603	83,165	13,111	—
Michigan	157,780	80,974	227,817	8,848	920
Minnesota	80,722	22,138	103,381	7,110	9,720
Mississippi	12,233	61,589	67,068	700	—
Missouri	108,256	24,934	90,766	6,215	—

Montana	7,933	2,284	2,905	871	—
Nebraska	38,170	4,302	40,197	2,083	1,850
Nevada	4,037	418	—0—	129	—
New Hampshire	17,570	6,306	25,854	1,987	4,750
New Jersey	233,207	21,244	206,829	27,773	—
New Mexico	9,921	4,149	8,187	—0—	—
New York	589,129	97,785	726,527	39,613	96,200
No. Carolina	11,634	19,469	—0—	1,134	—
No. Dakota	10,701	1,237	6,960	276	—
Ohio	260,447	11,729	276,717	18,921	31,600
Oklahoma	8,088	4,401	—0—	84	—
Oregon	16,430	6,783	21,050	1,528	—
Pennsylvania	401,649	42,067	265,257	35,985	48,000
Rhode Island	28,314	4,400	31,206	2,479	1,800
So. Carolina	7,425	26,157	7,085	750	—
So. Dakota	8,076	6,628	10,711	1,467	—
Tennessee	17,461	21,171	32,290	—0—	—
Texas	86,022	35,989	111,271	2,210	—
Utah	2,905	1,380	—0—	269	—
Vermont	5,211	5,041	11,452	902	1,050
Virginia	25,577	43,936	62,689	1,044	—
Washington	28,574	13,573	18,836	3,899	—
West Virginia	9,813	1,087	11,264	364	828
Wisconsin	137,437	44,557	188,325	7,820	16,800
Wyoming	2,143	115	1,335	—0—	—

[a]Estimated as follows: actual 1970-71 enrollments were increased by 4.4 percent in the Northeast, 8.8 percent in the Great Lakes, Plains, West, and Southwest, and by 13.2 percent in the Southeast. These rates are consistent with the differential regional rates of growth for the previous two years, as reported in *NCES Bulletin*, no. 12 (June 7, 1972), and consistent with the overall national increase in these enrollments from 1970-71 to 1972-73, as reported in U.S. Bureau of the Census, *Current Population Reports*, Series P-20, nos. 222 and 243, p. 3 in each.

[b]Assumption I is that all nonpublic students transfer to the public schools in 1972-73. Excess calculated as column (1) plus column (2) minus column (5) of Table 4B-1.

[c]Calculated as the number of transfers from Catholic schools; net transfers from other schools are assumed to be negligible.

[d]Assumption II is that the actual number of transfers increases to 20 percent.

Sources: Total Catholic Enrollment and Catholic transfers from National Catholic Education Association, *U.S. Catholic Schools, 1972-73* (Washington: NCEA Research Department, 1973), Table 1-6; Non-Catholic Nonpublic enrollment from *NCES Bulletin*, no. 12 (June 7, 1972); Table 2, p. 5.

Table 4B-3

Estimated Marginal Cost of Absorbing Nonpublic Students into the Public Schools, 1972-73

	(1) Avg. Annual Teacher Salary, 1972-73	(2) Nonteacher Salary Cost Adjustment[a]	(3) Pupil-Teacher Ratio	(4) Estimated Marginal Cost 1972-73[b]
Alabama	8,105	1.52	23.9	516
Alaska	14,491	1.55	21.4	1,050
Arizona	10,460	1.50	22.6	694
Arkansas	7,508	1.43	22.0	488
California	11,760	1.55	27.0	675
Colorado	9,744	1.50	23.4	626
Connecticut	10,600	1.52	20.5	786
Delaware	10,610	1.55	21.8	755
Florida	9,220	1.55	22.8	627
Georgia	8,204	1.55	22.9	556
Hawaii	10,700	1.55	22.8	727
Idaho	7,657	1.50	23.7	485
Illinois	11,200	1.45	21.4	759
Indiana	9,856	1.45	22.5	635
Iowa	9,645	1.48	20.1	710
Kansas	8,499	1.48	18.9	666
Kentucky	7,825	1.52	23.8	500
Louisiana	9,094	1.43	21.5	605
Maine	8,988	1.52	22.1	618
Maryland	11,159	1.55	22.2	780
Massachusetts	10,520	1.52	22.2	720
Michigan	11,950	1.45	24.6	704
Minnesota	10,526	1.48	21.1	738
Mississippi	6,924	1.52	23.6	446
Missouri	9,074	1.48	24.6	546

Montana	8,908	1.50	20.2	661
Nebraska	8,730	1.48	19.5	663
Nevada	10,882	1.50	24.9	655
New Hampshire	9,045	1.52	21.9	628
New Jersey	11,230	1.60	20.5	876
New Mexico	8,452	1.50	23.6	537
New York	12,380	1.60	19.4	1,021
No. Carolina	9,076	1.55	23.9	539
No. Dakota	8,101	1.48	20.7	632
Ohio	9,300	1.45	22.9	589
Oklahoma	7,866	1.43	22.2	507
Oregon	9,567	1.55	21.7	683
Pennsylvania	10,600	1.60	21.6	785
Rhode Island	10,326	1.52	20.6	762
So. Carolina	8,005	1.55	23.1	537
So. Dakota	7,908	1.48	20.1	582
Tennessee	8,305	1.52	25.0	505
Texas	8,735	1.43	21.1	592
Utah	8,560	1.50	26.5	485
Vermont	8,610	1.52	17.5	748
Virginia	9,596	1.55	20.8	715
Washington	10,582	1.55	24.1	681
W. Virginia	8,183	1.55	24.7	513
Wisconsin	10,423	1.45	18.9	799
Wyoming	9,500	1.50	18.6	766

[a]Calculated as 1 plus the percent that total nonteacher salary costs within the state are of total teacher salary costs in that state (data used were actually regional, there being nine regions in all). Latest state-by-state data is for 1968-69. Analysis of it suggests that within a given region there is little variation among the states—see U.S. Office of Education, *Statistics of Local Public School Systems, Finances 1968-69* (Washington: U.S. Government Printing Office, 1971), Table 5, pp. 182-202.

[b]Calculated as column (1) times column (2) divided by column (3).

Sources: Teacher Salaries from National Education Association, *Estimates of School Statistics, 1972-73* (NEA Research Report no. 1972-R12), Table 8, p. 31; Non-Teacher-Salary adjustment from Orlando F. Furno and Paul K. Cunco, "Cost of Education Index, 1972-73," *School Management 17*, no. 1 (January 1973): 14; Pupil-teacher ratio: see Table 4B-10.

Table 4B-4
Estimated per Pupil Cost of School Construction, 1972-73

(1) State	*(2)* Per Pupil Cost	*(3)* State	*(4)* Per Pupil Cost
Alabama	1,066	Montana	1,615
Alaska	2,739	Nebraska	1,711
Arizona	1,269	Nevada	3,333
Arkansas	896	New Hampshire	2,500
California	1,523	New Jersey	2,738
Colorado	1,249	New Mexico	1,088
Connecticut	3,533	New York	3,250
Delaware	2,457	No. Carolina	1,447
Florida	1,670	No. Dakota	833
Georgia	1,667	Ohio	1,637
Hawaii	2,533	Oklahoma	1,119
Idaho	1,307	Oregon	1,934
Illinois	2,260	Pennsylvania	2,695
Indiana	2,246	Rhode Island	4,230
Iowa	1,541	So. Carolina	1,098
Kansas	1,854	So. Dakota	1,417
Kentucky	1,462	Tennessee	1,914
Louisiana	1,068	Texas	1,131
Maine	1,794	Utah	1,756
Maryland	2,235	Vermont	1,500
Massachusetts	3,878	Virginia	1,445
Michigan	2,103	Washington	2,062
Minnesota	1,858	West Virginia	1,707
Mississippi	563	Wisconsin	1,874
Missouri	1,353	Wyoming	1,346

Source: "12th Annual Cost of Building Index (1972-73)," *School Management* 17, no. 5 (June/July 1973): 16-27. (Figure used was for "New Elementary" which seemed most representative of all construction.)

5

Public Policy for Existing Nonpublic Schools

I am irrevocably committed to these propositions: America needs her nonpublic schools. Those nonpublic schools need help . Therefore, we must and will find ways to provide that help.

Richard Nixon
(Philadelphia, April 6, 1972)

There are actually two fiscal issues involved in the question of public aid to existing nonpublic schools. The first deals with the burden of finance: who should pay what part of the cost of nonpublic schooling? The second concerns the impact that rising costs are having: what part of enrollment declines or school shutdowns may be attributed to increased costs? From a policy perspective, these issues may be reformulated as (1) is there a rationale for public support of the nonpublic schools; and (2) would additional support have an impact on nonpublic enrollments or the number of nonpublic schools.

As outlined in Chapter 4, America's nonpublic schools are alleged to provide three types of benefits to the general public: (1) economic, in reducing the cost of public schooling; (2) social, in helping to maintain stable integrated neighborhoods and in providing choice to parents; and (3) educational, in stimulating innovations in schooling through competition. However, it was shown that the available evidence supports the second and the third allegations only for a handful of nonpublic schools.[a] More importantly, perhaps, it was also shown that there is little merit to the belief that aiding existing nonpublic schools will save the taxpayers money, except possibly in a few local areas. Only in the unlikely event of a total, or near total, immediate collapse might absorbing students prove more costly. For the $1 billion annual subsidy it would take simply to eliminate operating deficits in the nonpublic schools and hence avoid additional cost increases—that is, to keep students from transferring because of new price rises or school closings—the public schools could absorb about half of all nonpublic students in the current year. More probable scenarios yield considerably smaller costs of absorption (see Chapter 4).

Nevertheless, the president and powerful members of Congress seem to

---

[a]Even here it is not clear that the same objectives might not better be achieved through the public schools.

feel that the case for aid is a valid one (see Chapter 1). For the most part, their focus has remained on the large operating deficits of the existing nonpublic schools and on what steps the government could take to eliminate these deficits. Even should the political forces favoring aid prevail, they must face the second issue: what will work? As Chapter 2 showed, much of the decline in the nonpublic sector is a result of taste and demographic factors. As a result, while preventing schools from closing might be feasible, completely eliminating this decline in enrollments might prove unobtainable, except at the expense of either very high per pupil subsidies which would divert funds from public school programs,[b] or through a substantial restructuring of the public school system. Moreover, if aid is targeted in line with the social and educational rationales that have been presented, it will do little or nothing for most existing nonpublic schools —notwithstanding whether it generates the alleged benefits.

Even so, a number of alternative programs for aid to these schools have been put forth, the most comprehensive being that of the President's Panel on Nonpublic Education. This chapter will examine these proposals and the possible alternatives in the context of the two fiscal issues noted above and in light of the rationale and evidence presented in earlier chapters. It will also try to indicate the constitutional implications of the various alternatives, as they are likely to be interpreted by the present Supreme Court. By the way of background, the chapter first considers the existing system of public aid, and what steps the nonpublic schools might take without additional legislation.

The Present System

While public assistance constitutes only a very small fraction of the budgets of the existing nonpublic schools, there in fact currently exists a number of vehicles for aid, both direct and indirect, which in all constitute a very substantial system of aid.

Virtually all government expenditures, or direct aid to nonpublic schools, are in the form of specific categories of assistance.[c] Most direct expenditures come from state governments. Thirty-seven of the fifty states provide one or more categorical aid programs—some states have as many as seven such programs. Estimating the total amount of these expenditures is difficult because frequently they are part of a single program for both public and nonpublic school students, and separate accounting records for the two groups of schools are not kept. However, calculations based on a

[b]The higher the subsidies to nonpublic schools, the more people there are likely to be who wish to take advantage of them, with the possible result that if aid is sufficient to maintain Catholic enrollments, it will actually lead to overall increased enrollments in nonpublic schools.

[c]Direct general aid has usually been found to violate either the state or federal constitutions.

Table 5-1

Public Aid to Nonpublic Schools and Total Income of Nonpublic Schools, Fiscal Year 1971

Type of Aid and Income Item	Amount (Millions)	Percentage of Total
Federal Aid		
Direct Expenditures	99.4	4.0
Income Tax Deductions	126.3	5.1
Total	225.7	9.2
State Aid		
Direct Expenditures	207.7	8.5
Income Tax Deductions	6.3	0.3
Total	214.0	8.7
Local Aid		
Direct Expenditures	2.1	0.1
Property Tax Exemptions	207.4	8.4
Total	209.5	8.5
Total Public Aid		
Direct Expenditures	309.2	12.6
Tax Deductions/Exemptions	340.0	13.8
Total	649.2	26.4
Total Income Plus Nonreported Public Aid and Subsidies	2,455.7	100.0

Sources: Direct expenditures from *Public Aid to Nonpublic Education,* a study prepared by the staff of the President's Commission on School Finance (Washington, 1971). Local expenditures are estimated as 1 percent of state expenditures. For estimation of tax subsidies, see notes 12 and 13. State income tax estimated as 5 percent of federal income tax.

survey by the staff of the President's Commission on School Finance suggest that in 1970-71 state direct aid programs to nonpublic schools totaled approximately $208 million, $84 million of which was expended by New York State[1] (see Table 5-1). The largest single item was the provision of transportation services—it accounted for over one-fourth of total expenditures. Assistance for handicapped children accounted for another one-fifth of the total. Among the wide variety of programs constituting the remaining expenditures,[d] three programs have recently been declared unconstitutional by either state or federal courts (see Appendix 4A). These three, which accounted for a third of total expenditures in 1970-71, were purchase of secular services, teacher salary supplements, and administrative services reimbursement. Still, total appropriations were up somewhat for 1971-72, second 1972-73 as more states added more programs, as existing programs were expanded, and as states affected by the courts

[d]Which include tax adjustments, dual enrollment, lease of facilities, equipment grants, text book aid, driver education, nutrition programs, and health services.

sought to rechannel funds into as yet unchallenged programs. Most existing state programs, especially those which have successfully withstood court tests, might better be viewed as "child welfare" programs rather than "educational" ones—that is, their principal focus is the child's physical safety and welfare, not directly aiding the school process. Because such programs can provide only very limited funding, recently some states have sought to initiate general aid programs, designed to hold down parental costs. Connecticut, for example, enacted a law in 1972 providing parents of nonpublic school students with $75 annually for each elementary school child and $150 for each secondary school child.[2] Similar laws in Ohio and Pennsylvania, however, have recently been struck down by the Supreme Court (see Appendix 4A).

Direct local government assistance is generally similar in type and variety to state government aid, although it is more scattered and irregular.[e] There is virtually no data with which to determine the amount of this aid; but it is generally believed to be only a small fraction of the sums budgeted by state governments—in Table 5-1 it is estimated as 1 per cent of state expenditures. As noted earlier, the state and local total of over $228 million is considerably higher than the $40 million or so reported as income by nonpublic schools. The vast part of this aid is not administered by these schools. Some of it is given directly to parents or students. Much of it is given as "in kind" aid. Dual enrollment programs, for example, which exist in thirty-three states, involve no transfer of funds.[f] The same is true for shared facilities and services programs and for many pupil transportation plans.[3] As a consequence, this assistance does not enter into the schools' budgets.

Direct federal aid is limited to a few programs, most of which differ from state and local programs. In 1970-71 the U.S. Office of Education estimates it contributed about $100 million to nonpublic schools (Table 5-1). Of this sum, about 44 percent was for aid to students from disadvantaged backgrounds (ESEA, Title I) and another one-third was for school food programs. The remainder went to aid for purchasing books, equipment, and supplementary services (ESEA, Title III). Similar to state and local aid, less than half of total federal aid appears in the budgets of nonpublic schools.[g]

Indirect public aid for nonpublic schools comes from the government

---

[e]Distinguishing between state programs and local programs is often times arbitrary because local school districts usually administer the programs, for some or all of which they are reimbursed by the state.

[f]Under such a program, students take some courses in the public school and some in the nonpublic school—generally the more expensive programs are taught in the public school. Release-time and shared-facilities programs are variants of this same general approach.

[g]The principal omitted item is Title I of ESEA, which is administered by the local public school district.

abstaining from taxation: nonpublic schools are generally exempt from local property taxes and charitable contributions made either to churches or directly to nonpublic schools are deductible from income subject to federal and state income taxes. These indirect subsidies are often overlooked—not only do the schools not count them as income; but the respective governments do not count them as expenditures. However, these subsidies do reduce total operating expenditures and lower the tuitions of nonpublic schools, and hence they should be considered as a form of aid.[4]

The total value of these indirect tax subsidies is not readily available. However, calculations based on a sample of the various types of nonpublic schools and the average property-tax rate suggest that these exemptions totaled over $200 million in fiscal 1972.[5] In the same year, subsidies as a result of the deductibility of charitable contributions from federally taxable income amounted to an additional $126.3 million.[6] Reductions in state income-tax liabilities for such contributions were estimated to add another $6.5 million to the total (see Table 5-1). Together, the exemptions from local property taxes and from federal and state income taxes amounted to $340 million in indirect subsidies, or 14 percent of the income and aid received by the nonpublic schools. Added to direct government aid, which totaled $310 million in 1970-71, one finds that the government provided over one-fourth of the total direct and indirect income of the nonpublic schools, not an insubstantial role.

Within the framework of this present system, there would seem to be a number of ways for the existing nonpublic schools to strengthen their fiscal position and/or eliminate their operating deficit. The first is to take fuller advantage of aid for which they are already eligible, especially from the federal government. For example, only a third of all Catholic schools are currently participating in the National School Lunch Program and about three-fifths of the schools receive federal funds for library services.[7] Both of these are programs for which all schools are eligible. Similarly, Catholic schools eligible for assistance under Title I of ESEA are not taking full advantage of the provisions of the law.[8] The low reported income from federal programs by other nonpublic schools suggests that their participation rates are equally low.[9] While public school officials, who technically administer federal programs, can make participation difficult for the nonpublic schools,[h] these low participation rates can easily be overcome by the various national associations, with which the schools are affiliated, providing their respective schools with better information on program regulations.

There would also seem to be room for nonpublic schools to participate

[h]This is largely because there are not separate funds for the exclusive use of the nonpublic schools, but rather a common set of funds which must be shared.

more extensively in state and local programs. School officials could take the lead in setting up additional dual enrollment or shared time programs in those states that have authorized such programs.[10] However, implementation of these programs may not ease the financial problems of the nonpublic schools. First, such schemes are impractical at the elementary level, where a class generally has a single teacher for all subjects. Second, particularly for sectarian institutions, a split program might actually reduce enrollments as parents begin to doubt the uniqueness which these schools claim as their reason for existing in the first place.[11] Greater participation in the various "child welfare" programs now established would not encounter these difficulties but likely would provide only marginal fiscal help.

Many nonpublic schools are also in a position to help themselves aside from additional public assistance. School consolidation, particularly among sectarian schools, would appear to be a significant way to achieve economies. For the most part, individual schools are virtually autonomous, with only minimal central administration—this is especially true at the elementary level, where decision-making power rests with the parishes. A systematic consolidation of Catholic schools, for example, could save many dioceses considerable sums—it has been estimated that on a national basis, total consolidation would by 1975 save the Catholic schools nearly one billion dollars annually, or over one-third of the total estimated operating costs for that year without consolidation.[12] A similar potential exists among Lutheran schools. Mergers have proceeded slowly, however. Parish pastors and their parishoners have been reluctant to give up their autonomy by combining with other parishes, with the result that many schools have been kept open with only partially filled classrooms.[13]

In addition, more centralized diocesan control or greater coordination among the schools could also generate important benefits through the redistribution of parish resources. Currently parishes must, for the most part, stand or fall on their own. Similar to the public schools, the net result is that wealthier parishes exert less effort and generally have lower tuitions, than do poorer parishes.[14] A central administration, however, could eliminate these disparities and be a vehicle for the wealthier parishes helping those with fiscal difficulties. In addition to redistributing revenues, Catholic and other sectarian schools might help themselves through increased tuitions or church subsidies. As was shown in Chapter 2, the price elasticity of demand is very small for these schools, especially at the low levels of tuition charged by many of them. The possibilities for additional church subsidies may be more limited, since total church revenues have risen little in recent years and little future increase is expected.[15] The substitutability of these two sources in the eyes of parishoners may also limit potential gains here. A study in Philadelphia, for example, showed that when tuitions were raised, parish collections declined by a similar amount.[16] However, it would seem that a shift away from tuitions to tax-deductible contributions would result in increased total revenues for sectarian schools—for the same amount of total giving, more revenue is actually realized. But the greater uncertainty of this method may reduce its desirability.

Taken together these various means of self-help are likely to go a long way toward eliminating the current operating deficit of the Catholic and other nonpublic schools. They will do so, however, only at the expense of substantial school closings and additional declines in enrollment. They also are likely to help only at the expense of many sectarian schools ceasing to be the quasi-public institutions they have been since their inception—with considerably higher tuitions, many families may no longer be able to afford them. While both of these results might be efficient in a market context, they are precisely what proaid advocates seek to avoid. Hence political pressure for additional public support will likely continue; and the public debate will center on what form this aid should take.

Additional Public Assistance

As noted earlier, the most comprehensive proposal for additional public support is that of the President's Panel on Nonpublic Education. The four-point plan, which is detailed in Chapter 1's Appendix 1A, reflects an effort to avoid what the panel perceived as the limitations of the present system: it puts more emphasis on general rather than categorical aid, on indirect rather than direct aid, and on federal rather than state and local aid. Existing or new categorical aid programs appear to offer little opportunity for expanded government support. If the various "child welfare" programs—health, nutrition, transportation and textbook aid programs—were raised in all states to the level of New York State (currently the highest state by a wide margin), the total additional aid would be less than $200 million.[i] Moreover, educationally-oriented categorical programs (such as teacher salary supplements or the purchase of secular services) seem unable to pass constitutional tests.[j] The only new categorical aid program proposed by the panel is the subsidy involved in the proposed construction loans; and this subsidy is the least likely to withstand constitutional challenge since the buildings would in most cases be used for the teaching of religion.[17]

General aid given directly to the schools is also likely to be found unconstitutional. Hence the panel sought to channel virtually all of its

---

[i]Note, however, that such programs are likely to be much more efficient in generating social benefits than would a large program of general government support.

[j]For a discussion of the reasoning and criteria involved, see Appendix 4A.

proposed assistance to the students and their families. Both its proposals for aiding the urban poor and the tuition reimbursements, which it proposes be part of any future federal program, involve no funds being transferred directly to the schools. Who ultimately receives the benefit of this aid of course depends on what happens to tuitions. To the extent that they rise, aid is transferred from students' families to the school—and to the extent that this reduces church subsidies, the aid actually goes to the church. The largest item in the panel's proposal is even a more indirect form of aid: tax credits for nonpublic school tuitions. As noted earlier in Appendix 4A, while the economic effect of giving a person a cash grant or reducing that person's tax liability may be identical, the respective constitutional cases may be very different.[18] The tax credit proposal is an extension of the existing system of providing aid through relief from property and income taxes.

The third emphasis of the panel, to shift the major burden of finance from the state and local governments to the federal government, is in contrast to the proposals of its parent President's Commission on School Finance. That commission proposed that the states take over virtually all financing of the elementary and secondary schools and recommended only a temporary expansion in federal aid for public education. The panel's basic argument for this divergence is that the weak fiscal conditions of many states and their frequently stricter constitutions make them less suitable agents of subsidy.[19]

In considering the panel's proposal, two points stand out. First, the panel seems most concerned with forms of aid which will be deemed constitutional. Secondly, it seeks to find forms of aid which will raise large sums of money—and hence help eliminate the large operating deficits of the Catholic and other nonpublic schools. The logic of this approach seems to be a two-step process: once it is determined that the nonpublic schools provide public benefits, then this determination and the rationale for making it are ignored; the decision then is how much aid is necessary and what means are available. Little attention is given to the specific benefits these schools are alleged to provide, to which schools provide those benefits, and to whether benefits are less than costs or less than the benefits that would be derived from a similar program in the public schools. The panel's proposals to aid the inner-city poor (see Appendix 1A) seem to be its one effort to take specific account of alleged benefits. By the panel's own estimation, however, this will be a very small program.[20] Moreover, no consideration is given to whether the poor might better be served by, for example, a comparable expansion of ESEA, Title I—which in fact can be used in both public and nonpublic schools. Their concern seems to be more with keeping open the nonpublic schools.[21]

The panel's largest proposals in terms of public aid dollars ignore alleged benefits altogether. As was shown in Chapter 4, except for a few localities perhaps, only by targeting aid on those about to leave for cost-related reasons or on schools about to close can subsidies to the nonpublic schools save the taxpayers money. The proposed tax credit and tuition reimbursement schemes (see below) involve no targeting at all, and hence would largely result in a windfall again either for many parents of nonpublic school pupils or for their respective schools and/or churches. Similarly, no effort is made by the panel to target funds to innovative programs or to innovative schools—as noted earlier, such a program would likely be small and hence of little value in the panel's logic. Finally, as noted earlier, because of the high concentration of nonpublic school pupils in a few states and localities, the federal government would seem to be the least appropriate government to provide aid. There would seem to be a conflict between finding ways which are constitutionally acceptable, and attempting to provide public support for the specific public benefits these schools are alleged to provide.

As a matter of national policy, the President's Panel believes it is of paramount importance that parents have a choice of schools to which to send their children. In Chapter 3 it was shown that this might in fact be a criterion for a program of general aid. However, as shown in Chapter 4, even with large federal subsidies this choice would likely be available only to a small fraction of the population, particularly with the sectarian nature of most existing nonpublic schools is taken into account, and the choice would really be one of which set of classmates would a student have.[k] Moreover, it was further shown that since many regard aid to sectarian schools as a serious disbenefit, the net benefits of a general aid program might be zero or negative.

The above discussion hinges very much on the continuance of the present institutional framework of our nation's elementary and secondary schools. As noted earlier, many people across the country are in fact arguing for a substantial reorganization of the education sector, specifically for some form of a universal voucher system.[22] A voucher system which included nonpublic schools would eliminate the current price differential between public and nonpublic schooling—making the issue of whether or not it is cheaper to absorb students irrelevant. A family, in deciding whether to switch from public to nonpublic schooling, would now only have to consider marginal costs and marginal benefits. This would likely lead to considerable expansion of the nonpublic sector and to its becoming a real source of choice. Nonpublic schools, sectarian and nonsectarian, would survive or fail on the basis of their perceived unique educational

---

[k]As the Coleman Report and others have shown, this is not an unimportant choice. However, given the public goods nature of the choice, it is not clear that improving the market will improve social welfare.

value. If sectarian schools, however, are not included in the voucher plan for constitutional reasons, these schools—the bulk of existing nonpublic schools—will likely be even worse off financially. In addition for the plan to work, it will have to stimulate diversification in the public sector or considerable expansion of the nonsectarian portion of the nonpublic sector. Opponents of voucher plans believe that the benefits gained from increased choice and diversity would be outweighed by the costs to society resulting from a lessening of the socialization outputs of the schools.[1] Moreover, a program which does not include the sectarian schools is likely to find itself with little political support. As a result, politicians are likely to continue to consider various tax schemes, despite their seeming unrelatedness to the public welfare.

As noted in Chapter 1, a number of tax proposals have been introduced in Congress. The vast majority have involved tax credits for payment of nonpublic school tuitions. The particular plan receiving the most attention is the one introduced by Congressmen Mills and Carey, and endorsed by the administration.[23] It would provide a federal income tax credit of 50 percent for tuitions paid to nonprofit private institutions—up to $400 of tuition—with a gradual phasing out of the credit for families with income over $18,000. Such a program, it is estimated would have provided $350 million in benefits in 1972-73 (see Table 5-2). This figure presumes no rise in current tuition levels, somewhat unrealistically. If all tuitions rose to the $400 ceiling in the bill, the cost of the program would double.[24]

There are a number of objections to this plan. The first is that the poor, who have no tax liabilities, receive no benefits. This might be overcome by giving a rebate to those with insufficient tax liabilities—even so, families with incomes under $5,000 would have received only $5.5 million in 1972-73. Moreover, many believe this would make the plan unconstitutional because it would be more like a tuition grant.[m] A second objection to the plan is that it represents a perverse redistribution of income, one of the arguments against aid made Chapter 4. Even with the phaseout provision, the bulk of the benefits would go to families with above average incomes. Finally, some persons doubt the constitutionality of any tax scheme, since there is no way to assure that this public aid will not be used to support religion.[25]

For this reason, some have proposed allowing tax *deductions* for nonpublic school tuitons. In effect, this would mean merely expanding the provisions of the tax code which now permit deductions for contributions

---

[1]Note that while some critics would praise a weakening of the socialization process, others would argue that there's little chance of it happening so long as the social relations of production remained unchanged.

[m]The general rule seems to be that the less directly the aid is tied to tuition, the more likely it is to be found constitutional. Hence making it some fraction of tuition rather than 100 percent, not having a rebate, and having a high-income cutoff all are seen as legal improvements.

Table 5-2
Estimated Effect of the Tuition Tax Credit under HR 17072 for the 1972-73 School Year

Adjusted Gross Income Class	Number of Nonpublic School Students (Thousands)	Average Tuition Paid	Amount of Tax Credit		Percentage Distribution of Total Tax Credit
			Per Pupil	Total (Millions)	
Under $3,000	94.2	$ 30	$ 0.0	$ 0.00	0.0
$3,000-$5,000	232.9	44	1.0	4.29	0.3
$5,000-$7,500	687.5	80	21.4	31.13	6.1
$7,500-$10,000	1,092.3	140	74.2	67.93	21.2
$10,000-$15,000	1,544.9	195	144.1	93.37	41.2
$15,00-$20,000	708.1	549	89.8	126.86	25.7
$20,000-$25,000	230.4	911	18.5	80.35	5.3
Over $25,000	268.2	1,038	1.0	3.77	0.3
Total	4,858.5	288	72.04	350.00	100.0

Source: Author's estimates based on Joint Committee on Internal Revenue Taxation, Staff Study on HR 13495, February 10, 1972. (It was assumed that tuitions were $400 or less per pupil for families with incomes under $15,000. For families with incomes between $15,000 and $30,000 authors' own estimates of distrubution of tuitions paid and average income within income classes were used; all families were assumed to have the average number of children for their income class. For families with incomes over $30,000 only those with four or more students in nonpublic schools would be eligible for a tax credit. The total amount of such grants was assumed to be negligible.)

to the churches or gifts to the schools.[26] While these plans are more likely to pass constitutionai tests,[n] since they are even more like income redefinition and less like tuition grants than tax credits, they are even more prorich than the tax credit scheme described above. The benefit any family would receive is equal to the tuition paid times its marginal tax rate. As a result, for example, the deductability of $400 in tuition would provide $144 in benefits to a family with $25,00 of taxable income, but only $76 to a family with $8,000 income. Moreover, only families actually itemizing deductions would benefit; and these are likely to be those with higher incomes.[27] Tax deduction plans also provide little aid in cases where schools, for social reasons, want to maintain low tuition levels. Catholic schools, for example, are expected to have tuition levels of about $150 by 1975.[28] At this level, introduction of a tax deductability scheme would permit tuitions to be increased $50 without increasing costs to the average parent.[o] However, such an increase would cover only 20 percent of the projected deficit.

Conclusion

The president and his Panel on Nonpublic Education have both asserted that nonpublic schools are a ''national asset'' and that hence these schools should be publicly aided. Where necessary they have assumed appropriate answers to the fiscal and educational issues involved. Then, once they decided in favor of aid, they have sought to obtain however much aid and through whatever form they thought possible. In this effort, they appear to have the support of a number of powerful politicians. I do not doubt that nonpublic schools are a valuable asset to that portion of the nation's families having their children enrolled in them. The issue, however, is whether these schools provide benefits for those families not having children enrolled and hence are deserving of their support.

In making such a determination, one important factor often overlooked by advocates of aid is the impact aid for nonpublic schools will have on the public school sector or on other government education policies. As has been noted previously, aid to the nonpublic schools would most likely divert funds from the public schools. Hence the benefits of any program of aid to the nonpublic schools must be compared with the loss in benefits from the foregone aid to public schools. In view of the priority currently given, at least in the federal budget, to aiding the poor and enhancing equal educational opportunity, it seems unlikely that a program providing assis-

---

[n]Deductions are even less tied to tuition than are credits. See note m.

[o]This assumes that all families with children in these schools can take advantage of the deduction, and that the average family will have a taxable income in 1975 of $13,000. Hence this is probably an upper limit estimate.

tance largely to families with above average incomes would be consistent with this priority.[p] Moreover, given that parental choice appears to be the rationale used to justify a program of general aid to nonpublic schools, and that presently at least that choice is largely one of which classmates a child will have, such a program would be consistent with the public good only if it makes either the availability of that choice or the collective outcome of such choices independent of race or socioeconomic status. Finally, a general aid program such as the proposed tax credits for tuition may alter the very structure of the public schools, as they seek to capture some of this aid. While charging tuitions is counter to a long tradition in the public schools, it is hard to imagine school administrators passing up this opportunity for general federal support, something they do not now receive.[q] In the long run, this program may prove to be the first step toward a universal voucher system for education, the end product of which is likely to be a large expansion of privately operated schools.

Even should the public pay for all of the alleged public benefits of the existing nonpublic schools, it is not clear what this will do for the future viability of these schools. Tuitions will still certainly have to rise substantially in Catholic and other sectarian schools.[r] What the overall effect on enrollment will be is unclear; but it seems likely, barring any unforeseen change in the nature of the Catholic schools, that even with large federal assistance their enrollments will continue to decline. However, a large aid program may bring about substantial increases in nonsectarian nonpublic schools, thus dramatically changing the structure of the nonpublic sector. Nevertheless, unless these new schools differ widely, the real choice available to students will continue to be very limited; and unless their numbers increase substantially, their competitive value will continue to be limited.

Ultimately, the future of existing nonpublic schools may be affected more by what happens in the public-school sector than by a program of direct government aid. If proposed changes in the financing of the public schools such as complete state funding, which are designed to reduce inequities, result in reduced quality in some areas and/or in less choice and local autonomy, many people may opt out of the public schools in favor of nonpublic education. If, on the other hand, proposed changes lead to increased quality, choice and diversity within the public sector,[29] then no public program is likely to keep the nonpublic sector from shrinking sub-

---

[p]On the other hand, since stimulating innovations is also an important federal goal, a program aimed specifically at this end, while not providing the large funds of a general grant program, would be more consistent with federal educational objectives.

[q]I wish to thank Robert Hartman for pointing out this possibility to me.

[r]Aid programs that are tied to tuitions will create greater incentives for this to happen than will programs that are not.

stantially. In short, the viability of the nonpublic schools and their being deserving of public assistance, depend on these schools finding a truly unique role, from a public viewpoint, in American education; and determination of such a role can only be made in the context of entire schooling system. Much of the proaid rhetoric sounds like support for aid to nonpublic schools simply for the sake of nonpublic schools. From an economic viewpoint at least, in light of the available evidence, that is not sound public policy.

Notes

Chapter 1
Introduction

1. Richard Nixon, "Remarks of the President to the 69th Annual Convention National Catholic Education Association," Civic Center, Philadelphia, April 6, 1972, p. 7.

2. See the *Washington Post,* June 27, 1972, p. 2; and the *New York Times,* August 18, 1972.

3. U.S. President, "Executive Order No. 11513," March 3, 1970.

4. See *Weekly Compilation of Presidential Documents* (1970): 557-58.

5. Most of these bills provided for some form of tax credit to the parents of nonpublic school students. For a list of these bills, see *Material Relating to Proposals before the Committee on Ways and Means on the Subject of Aid to Primary and Secondary Education in the Form of Tax Credits and/or Deductions,* 92nd Cong., 2nd sess. (1972), p. III

6. U.S. Congress, House, H. R. 17072, "A Bill to Amend the Internal Revenue Code of 1954 to Allow a Credit against the Individual Income Tax for Tuition Paid for the Elementary and Secondary Education of Dependents," 92nd Cong., 2nd sess. (1972).

7. See Louis R. Gary, *The Collapse of Nonpublic Education: Rumor or Reality,* The Report on Nonpublic Education in the State of New York for the New York State Commission on the Quality, Cost and Financing of Elementary and Secondary Education (1972), vol. 2, pp. C-28 to C-100; also *Public Aid to Nonpublic Education,* a staff report of the President's Commission on School Finances (Washington: Commission, 1972).

8. National Education Association, *Resolutions and Other Actions* (Detroit: NEA Publications, July 1971), p. 9.

9. See "Statement of Andrew J. Biemiller, Director, Department of Legislation American Federation of Labor and Congress of Industrial Organization before the House Committee on Ways and Means on H. R. 16141, The Public and Private Education Assistance Act of 1972," Washington, September 6, 1972 (mimeographed).

10. See *Tax Aid for Parochial and Private Schools: A Compendium of Information for Debaters* (Silver Spring, Md.: American United Resource Foundation, August 1972), pp. 8-19.

11. See Eileen Shanahan, "2 Parties Push Nonpublic School with Bill for Tax Credits to Parents," *New York Times,* August 7, 1972, p. 19; also Louis R. Gary and K.C. Cole, "The Politics of Aid and a Proposal for Reform," in *Saturday Review of Education* 55 (July 22, 1972): 31-33.

12. See Kevin Phillips, *The Emerging Republican Majority* (New York: Arlington House, 1969), pp. 169-75; also "Vital Voting Bloc Defects to Nixon," *Washington Post,* October 8, 1972.

13. *Gallup Opinion Index,* no. 66 (December 1970), p.20, The poll also asked people whether or not they favored a voucher system which included nonpublic schools. The result was only slightly less favorable: 43 percent in favor and 46 percent opposed.

14. Ibid.

15. *Tax Aid for Parochial and Private Schools,* p. 35.

16. Ibid., pp. 35-36.

17. It is likely that those favoring aid have much stronger preferences than those who oppose it and that politicians are responding to this intensity of preference—see Anthony Downs, *An Economic Theory of Democracy* (New York: Harper and Row, 1957).

18. The President's Commission on School Finance, *Schools, People and Money* (Washington: U. S. Government Printing Office, 1972), p. ix.

19. In large cities the proportion was one-third. Source: *Gallup Opinion Index,* no. 81 (March 1972), p. 17.

20. See, for example, *Report of the New York State Commission on the Quality, Cost and Financing of Elementary and Secondary Education,* vol. 1 (New York: Commission, 1972).

21. See, for example, Charles Silberman, *Crisis in the Classroom: The Remaking of American Education* (New York: Random House, 1970), esp. chs. 3 and 4; also George Dennison, *The Lives of Children: The Story of the First Street School* (New York: Random House (Vintage Books), 1969, and Jonathan Kozol, *Death at an Early Age: The Destruction of the Hearts and Minds of Negro Children in the Boston Public Schools* (New York: Bantam Books, 1967).

22. Vivian T. Thayer, *Formative Ideas in American Education from the Colonial Period to the Present* (New York: Dodd, Mead and Company, 1965), pp. 94-97.

23. Ibid.

24. Lawrence Cremin, ed., *The Republic and the School: Horace Mann on the Education of Free Men,* Classics in Education no. 1 (New York: Teacher's College, Columbia University, 1957), pp. 89-91.

25. *Gallup Opinion Index,* no. 87 (September 1972), p. 18.

26. E.G. West, *Education and the State: A Study in Political Economy* (London: Institute of Economic Affairs, 1965), pp. 111 ff.

27. Milton Friedman, *Capitalism and Freedom* (Chicago: University of Chicago Press, 1962), p. 86.

28. Burton A. Weisbrod, "Education and Investment in Human Capital," *Journal of Political Economy* 70 (October 1962—part 2): 119. Weisbrod also notes that widespread use of such things as credit cards and checking accounts, as well as our system of income tax filing, would be severely limited by illiteracy.

29. West, *Education and the State,* p. 119.

30. Most people trace the start of this literature to T.W. Schultz, "Investment in Human Capital," *American Economic Review* 51 (February 1961):1-17. Schultz has subsequently written several books and articles on the subject. Perhaps the most often cited work is Gary S. Becker, *Human Capital: A Theoretical and Empirical Analysis with Special Reference to Education* (New York: National Bureau of Economic Research, 1964). A representative collection of readings may be found in B.F. Kiker, ed., *Investment in Human Capital* (Columbia, S.C.: University of South Carolina Press, 1971); and W. Lee Hansen, ed., *Education, Income and Human Capital*, Conference on Education and Income (New York: National Bureau of Economic Research, 1970).

31. See Burton A. Weisbrod, *External Benefits of Public Education: An Economic Analysis* (Princeton: Industrial Relations Section of Princeton University, 1964), pp. 33-34.

32. Vivian T. Thayer, *American Education,* pp. 105-106.

33. Ibid., p. 111. It should be noted that some churches, particularly the Roman Catholic, saw the school as the most appropriate institution for religious instruction and hence established their own school system.

34. *Abington School District* v. *Schempp,* 374 U.S. 203 (1963).

35. *Epperson* v. *Arkansas,* 393 U.S. 97 (1968). Such teaching had been opposed by members of the "fundamentalist" religions.

36. Nixon, "Remarks," p. 7.

37. As Charles Benson points out, parents, teachers, and other school officials all have varying preferences, and this becomes a significant problem in a large school system which serves a wide range of people—see Charles S. Benson "Economic Analysis of Institutional Alternatives for Providing Education (Public, Private Sector)," in Roe L. Johns et at., *Economic Factors Affecting the Financing of Education* (Gainsville: National Education Finance Project, 1970), pp. 122-24.

38. See Bowles, "Unequal Education"; also Herbert Gintis, "Education and the Characteristics of Worker Productivity," *American Economic Review* 61 (May 1971):266-79.

39. See Michael Katz, *The Irony of Early School Reform* (Cambridge: Harvard University Press, 1968); also Samuel S. Bowles, "Unequal Education and the Reproduction of the Social Division of Labor," *The Review*

of Radical Political Economics 3 (Fall/Winter 1971):1-30. Bowles points out how mass education first arose in the most industrialized areas, and then spread as industry spread (ibid., p. 7).

40. See previous note; also Samuel S. Bowles, "Schooling and Inequality from Generation to Generation," *Journal of Political Economy* 80 (May/June 1972). Some critics go even farther, arguing that while equal educational opportunity is a desirable goal, the schools are the least appropriate social institution to achieve that goal—see Ivan Illich, *Deschooling Society* (New York: Harper & Row, 1971), pp. 14-16.

41. See "Education for Docility," Chapter 3 in Silberman, *Crisis in the Classroom;* Silberman believes that this is a serious failing because students entering the schools today may still be in the labor force in the year 2030, performing jobs which do not exist today (pp. 114-15). John Holt and others argue similarly that what is more important is teaching students how to learn—see John Holt *What Do I Do on Monday* (New York: E.P. Dutton & Co., 1970).

42. See George Dennison, *Lives of Children,* pp. 5-6; also Jonathan Kozol, *Death at an Early Age,* pp. 179-83. For a critical review of these and similar authors, see Harvy Averch et at., *How Effective is Schooling: A Critical Review and Synthesis of Research Findings,* Final Report to the President's Commission on School Finance (Santa Monica: Rand Corporation, 1971), Ch. 7, pp. 126-47. Averch makes the point that these authors generally believe, "that the nature of the school experience is a dominant factor that determines not only how well cognitive skills are acquired, but also how effectively they can be used after school" (p. 126).

43. See Samuel Bowles and Herbert Gintis, "I.Q. in the U.S. Class Structure," *Social Policy* (November/December 1972-January/February 1973), pp. 65-96.

44. See Martin Katzman, *The Political Economy of Urban Schools* (Cambridge: Harvard University Press, 1971): also Jesse Burkhead, *Input and Output in a Large City High School* (Syracuse: Syracuse University Press, 1967). For a discussion of the related problem of false job expectations of students, see Ivar Berg, *The Great Training Robbery* (New York: Praeger Publishers, 1970).

45. See Samuel Bowles, "Toward an Education Production Function," in Hansen, *Education, Income and Human Capital,* pp. 11-60.

46. See Benson, "Economic Analysis," pp. 124-27.

47. See Irene A. King, *Bond Sales for Public School Programs, 1970-71* (Washington: U.S. Office of Education, National Center for Educational Statistics, 1972), pp. 2-3.

48. For a discussion of this pressure, see Robert D. Reischauer and

Robert W. Hartman with the assistance of Daniel J. Sullivan, *Reforming School Finance* (Washington: Brookings Institution, 1973), Ch. 3.

49. That is, just what is it we are trying to equalize? See, for example, James S. Coleman, "The Concept of Equality of Educational Opportunity," *Harvard Educational Review* 38 (Winter 1968): 7-22; also Samuel Bowles, "Towards Equality," ibid., pp. 89-99.

50. Silberman, *Crisis in the Classroom*, pp. 53-54.

51. Ibid. p. 81.

52. Ibid., pp. 70-112. On the effect of teacher expectations, see R.C. Rist, "Student Social Class and Teacher Expectations: The Self-Fulfilling Prophecy in Ghetto Education," *Harvard Educational Review* 40 (1970):411-51.

53. See Averch et al., *How Effective is Schooling*, pp. 129-31.

54. See Bowles and Gintis, "I.Q." These authors argue that a large failure in the above critics analyses is separating "equality of opportunity" from "equality of outcome." (pp. 91-92).

55. The initial work on this issue was Arthur E. Wise, *Rich Schools, Poor Schools: The Promise of Equal Educational Opportunity,* (Chicago: University of Chicago Press, 1968); see also, for example, Charles S. Benson, "Economic Analysis," pp. 127-28.

56. There has been a recent rapid growth in the literature on this issue. The focal work is John E. Coons et al., *Private Wealth and Public Education* (Cambridge: Bellnap Press of Harvard University Press, 1970); see also Reischauer and Hartman with Sullivan, *Reforming School Finance,* Ch. 4 and the second section of the bibliography.

57. The first of these cases, and the model on which the others are based was *Serrano* v. *Priest,* California Supreme Court 938254, L.A. 29820 (1971); subsequently, decisions were handed down in Minnesota, New Jersey, Texas, Wyoming, Arizona, and Kansas.

58. That was the Texas case: *Rodriguez* v. *San Antonio Independent School District,* Civil Action 68-175-SA, U.S. District Court, Western District of Texas, San Antonio Division (1971).

59. This typology is presented in Martin Katzman, *Political Economy of Urban Schools,* pp. 2-3.

60. See U.S. Dept. of Health, Education and Welfare, *The Effectiveness of Compensatory Education: Summary and Review of the Evidence* (Washington, DHEW, April 1972); also Averch et al., *How Effective is Schooling,* Ch. 6, pp. 100-25. For an alternative interpretation of why liberal social reform failed, see Bowles and Gintis, "I.Q." pp. 90-93.

61. Silberman, *Crisis in the Classroom,* Ch. 5; see also Anthony G.

Oettinger with the collaboration of Sema Marks, *Run, Computer, Run: The Mythology of Educational Innovation*, Studies in Technology and Society no. 58 (Cambridge: Harvard University Press, 1970).

62. See, for example, Katzman, *Political Economy of Urban Schools;* Burkhead, *Large City High Schools;* and Samuel S. Bowles, "Towards an Educational Production Function" (for an extensive list of input-output studies that have been done, see Averch et al., *How Effective is Schooling,* Appendix A.)

63. Charles Benson, "Economic Analysis," p. 126.

64. Averch et al., *How Effective Is Schooling,* p.xi.

65. James S. Coleman, "Incentives in Education, Existing and Proposed," Johns Hopkins University, 1970 (mimeo.); see also Benson, "Economic Analysis," pp. 121-22, and Charles Silberman, *Crisis in the Classroom,* pt. 3.

66. For a thorough discussion of various decentralization alternatives and their implications, see Henry M. Levin, *Community Control of Schools* (Washington: Brookings Institution, 1969).

67. Note that such discussion is limited to the conventional paradigm of schooling. It ignores radical educational alternatives such as those suggested by Illich, *Deschooling Society* and Everett Reimer, *School is Dead: Alternatives in Education* (Garden City: Doubleday, 1971).

68. Benson, "Economic Analysis," pp. 130-62.

69. Friedman, *Capitalism and Freedom,* pp. 86-98.

70. See Averch et al., *How Effective Is Schooling,* pp. 129-31.

71. Edelson defines a communal good as "collectively provided, equally shared"; there is no implication of it being public or private in the Samuelson sense. See Noel M. Edelson, "Efficiency Aspects of Local School Finance: Comments and Extensions," in *Journal of Political Economy* 81 (January/February 1973): 159-64.

72. *Committee for Public Education and Religious Liberty et al.* v. *Nyquist et al.,* no. 72-694 (slip opinion), decided June 25, 1973.

Appendix 1A
Reports of the President's Commission on School Finance and President's Panel on Nonpublic Education

1. The President's Commission on School Finance, *Schools, People and Money* (Washington: U.S. Government Printing Office, 1972), p. 53.

2. Ibid., p. 54.

3. Ibid., p. 56.

4. "1. To study and evaluate the problems concerning nonpublic schools; 2. To report the nature of the crisis confronting nonpublic schools; 3. To make positive recommendations to the President for action which will be in the interest of our entire national educational system." President's Panel on Nonpublic Education, *Nonpublic Education and the Public Good* (Washington; U.S. Government Printing Office, 1972), p. 1.

5. The "crisis" is described in a one-page section of the summary called "Findings of Fact"—President's Panel, *Nonpublic Education,* p. 55.

6. Ibid., chs. 2, 3, and 4.

7. Ibid., p. 32.

8. Ibid., p. 34. The rationale for a federal program is based on the states being more legally constrained and having less fiscal capacity.

9. President's Commission on School Finance, *Schools, People and Money,* p. xi.

Chapter 2
The Current Nonpublic System

1. President's Panel on Nonpublic Education, *Nonpublic Education and the Public Good* (Washington: U.S. Government Printing Office, 1972), p. 8.

2. U.S. Bureau of the Census, Census of Population: 1970, *General Economic and Social Characteristics*, PC(1)-C, volumes for the respective states, Table 51.

3. Sources: Nonpublic school enrollments and population density from the U.S. Bureau of the Census, *Census of Population: 1970*; Catholic population from P.J. Kennedy & Sons, *The Official Catholic Directory 1970* (Kennedy 1970); and per capita income from *Survey of Current Business* (August 1972).

4. National Catholic Educational Association *U.S. Catholic Schools, 1973-74* (Washington: NCEA Research Department, 1974), p. 7.

5. U.S. Bureau of the Census, *Census of Population: 1970*, PC(1)-C 26, (Mississippi), Tables 102, 120.

6. National Catholic Education Association, "NCEA Standard School Survey Form (1972)," p. 2.

7. Religious teachers in Catholic schools received an average salary of $1,995 in 1970-71, while the average lay teacher earned $6,328. If religious teachers had been paid on the same basis as their lay counterparts, average per pupil expenditures in the Catholic schools would have been 31 percent

higher in 1970-71. Moreover, if both groups had been paid comparable public school salaries, costs would have been nearly 50 percent higher. (Source: estimated from NCEA, *U.S. Catholic Schools, 1970-71*, pp. 24, 32.)

8. Again there is substantial variation within the Catholic sector; while half of these schools charge less than $50 tuition—relying mainly on church subsidies—others charge over $1000. National Catholic Educational Association, *U.S. Catholic Schools, 1971-72* (Washington: NCEA Research Department, 1972), p. 18. Moreover, Lutheran tuitions are even more widely dispersed than are Catholic school tuitions.

9. See U.S. Catholic Conference, "To Teach as Jesus Did," U.S. Catholic Bishops Pastoral Message on Catholic Education, *Origins* 2 (November 23, 1972): 359-61.

10. The connection between tuitions and contributions is evidenced by a study in Philadelphia which showed that when tuitions were raised, contributions declined by a similar amount. (Source: John T. Gurash, Chairman, *The Report of the Archdiocesan Advisory Committee on the Financial Crisis of Catholic Schools in Philadelphia and Surrounding Counties*, Philadelphia: Committee, 1972, p. 20—hereafter referred to as the *Gurash Committee Report*.)

11. NCEA, *U.S. Catholic Schools, 1970-71*, p. 9.

12. Ibid., p. 10.

13. Al H. Senske, "School Statistics of the Lutheran Church —Missouri Synod, September 1973," Board of Parish Education, Lutheran-Church-Missouri Synod (St. Louis: Board, 1974; processed); National Association of Independent Schools, *NAIS Report*, no. 49 (February 1974), p. 2. For a breakdown of the changes in nonpublic school enrollment in New York by institutional affiliation, see Louis R. Gary and Associates, "The Collapse of Nonpublic Education: Rumor or Reality?" The Report on Nonpublic Education in the State of New York for the New York State Commission on the Quality, Cost and Financing of Elementary and Secondary Education (New York: Commission, 1971; processed), Volume 1, Table T-2, p. I-6.

14. See New York Department of City Planning, "Three Out of Ten: The Nonpublic Schools of New York City" (Department of City Planning, City of New York, March 1972; processed), p. 18.

15. Southeastern Public Education Project, American Friends Service Committee, "Survey of Private Schools Started in Mississippi Since the Passage of the 1964 Civil Rights Act," in *Equal Educational Opportunity: Part 3A–Desegregation under Law*, Hearings before the Senate Select Committee on Equal Educational Opportunity, 91 Cong., 2nd sess. (1970),

pp. 1196-98; and unpublished data from Education Section, U.S. Department of Justice, 1971. Data from the U.S. Department of Health, Education and Welfare on school age population and white enrollment in Southern public schools during this period also suggests that "white flight" has been a relatively small phenomenon.

16. NCEA, *U.S. Catholic Schools, 1973-74*, p. 17.

17. While enrollment has been falling over the last six years, the number of teachers actually increased from 1967 to 1971 and has only declined slightly in the last two years.

18. Ibid., pp. 26-27.

19. Ibid., pp. 28-29. In the public schools, there have been only a negligible number of teachers without B.A. degrees. The relative experience of the two groups has not changed over the past few years.

20. Ernest Bartell, unpublished correspondence, 1972.

21. See Louis R. Gary and K.C. Cole, "The Politics of Aid—And a Proposal for Reform," *Saturday Review* 55 (July 22, 1972): 31-33.

22. NCEA, *U.S. Catholic Schools, 1970-71*, p. 29. See also the *Gurash Committee Report*, pp. xvii and 14; and *Report of the New York State Commission on the Quality, Cost and Financing of Elementary and Secondary Education* (New York: Commission, 1972), vol. 1, p. 5.35.

23. Ernest Bartell et al., *Catholic Education in St. Louis: Allocation and Distribution of Human and Financial Resources* (Notre Dame: Office for Education Research, University of Notre Dame, 1970).

24. Kenneth M. Brown, *Catholic Education in Atlanta: An Economic Analysis* (Notre Dame: Office for Educational Research University of Notre Dame, 1971). Both this and the previous study used linear regression analysis similar to mine to control for other possible influences.

25. *Report of the New York State Commission on the Quality, Cost and Financing of Elementary and Secondary Education*, p. 5.23.

26. *Gurash Committee Report*, p. xx. Neither this study nor the Fleischman Commission Report used a formal model to derive their conclusions. Rather, both studies relied on simple correlations, selected examples, and the virtual nonexistence of tuition in most schools, Hence they offer little help in predicting what will happen if tuitions rise by significant amounts.

27. Kenneth M. Brown, "Enrollment in Nonpublic Schools," in Frank J. Fahey (Director), *Economic Problems of Nonpublic Schools*, submitted to the President's Commission on School Finance by the Office for Educational Research, University of Notre Dame (Commission, 1972), p. 178.

28. NCEA, *U.S. Catholic Schools, 1973-74*, p. 5.

29. Based on method in Brown, "Enrollment in Nonpublic Schools," pp. 164-65, and data from NCEA, *U.S. Catholic Schools, 1973-74*, p. 7.

30. NCEA, *U.S. Catholic Schools, 1973-74*, pp. 5-7. For example, although the number of parish elementary schools declined from 9817 to 7696, the number of interparochial and diocesan elementary schools rose from 169 to 534. In rural areas, many school closings have resulted from the consolidation of smaller schools and do not therefore necessarily imply enrollment decreases (ibid., pp. 8-9). In Buffalo, New York, when ten poorly attended schools were closed, the diocese made sure that all the children would be accommodated in other institutions in the diocese (George R. La Noue, "Parochial Schools and Public Policy," in Gary and Associates, "Collapse of Nonpublic Education," vol. 2, p. 2.).

31. During this period the average excess capacity in Catholic elementary schools was 53 spaces (estimated from NCEA, *U.S. Catholic Schools, 1971-72*, Table 37, p. 59). Assuming that for one-fourth to one-half of the schools that closed there was another school sufficiently close to which students could transfer (assumption based on the type of location of Catholic elementary schools—see Table 2-4), then 1800 schools x 53 x ¼ (½) yields 24,000 (48,000) students.

32. See Dennis J. Dugan, "The Determinants of Enrollment in Catholic Schools: An Empirical Analysis of the Archdiocese of St. Louis," in Fahey, *Nonpublic Schools*, pp. 421, 423.

33. These two factors are very highly correlated, see Dennis J. Dugan, "Determinants of Enrollment in Catholic Schools," p. 395.

34. See Frank J. Fahey and Richard G. Kiekbusch, "Attitudes Toward Nonpublic Education," in Fahey, *Nonpublic Schools*, pp. 1-154.

35. Unpublished data, collected as part of *The Catholic Education Study Report*, directed by George Elford, Superintendent of Schools, for the Archdiocese of Indianapolis (Archdiocese of Indianapolis, 1968). Figures in parentheses are results from the central cities; in both the cities and the suburbs, the large majority of Catholic parents sent their children to Catholic schools.

36. Brown, "Enrollment in Nonpublic Schools," p. 172. This probably explains why a higher fraction of suburban Catholic schools have closed in recent years than have central city schools.

37. See "Declaration on Christian Education (*Gravissimum Educationis*)," in Walter M. Abbot, S.J., ed, *The Documents of Vatican II* (New York: America Press, 1966), pp. 637-51 (esp. para. no. 3, pp. 641-42). Prior to this time, tremendous pressure was put on parents to enroll their children in Catholic schools—to not do so was considered virtually "sinful."

38. For a discussion of this, see George Elford, "School Crisis—or Parish Crisis?" *Commonweal* 93 (January 29, 1971): 418-20.

39. See Jack Rosenthal, "Study Shows Catholics Having Smaller Families," *New York Times*, May 30, 1972, pp. 1, 5. (The study referred to in the article is the 1970 National Fertility Study, submitted to the Commission on Population Growth and the American Future.)

40. Donald A. Erickson et al., "Crisis in Illinois Nonpublic Schools," Final Research Report to the Elementary and Secondary Nonpublic Schools Study Commission, State of Illinois (Commission, 1971; processed), p. 4-20.

41. See Arthur J. Corrazini, "The Non-Catholic Private School," in Fahey, *Nonpublic Schools*, p. 295.

42. In NAIS, schools, for example, costs have risen only 22 percent in the last three years (*NAIS Report*, nos. 35 (December 1970), 39 (January 1972) and 43 (January 1973).

43. The total is projected to fall from 80,312 in 1970 to 42,812 in 1975 and to 20,142 in 1980 (Ernest J. Bartell, "Costs and Revenues in Nonpublic Elementary and Secondary Education: The Past, Present and Future of Roman Catholic Schools," in Fahey, *Nonpublic Schools*, pp. 218, 563, 565). In New York, the number of religious order teachers is projected to decline from 12,542 in 1969-70 to 1,375 in 1980-81; Gary and Associates, "Collapse of Nonpublic Education," vol. 1, p. II-11. In both cases, three factors are combining to produce these extremely high rates of attrition: (1) the number of new entrants has become almost negligible; (2) people are quitting the religious life in ever greater numbers; and (3) some religious orders are de-emphasizing teaching and branching out into other activities.

44. See Bartell, "Costs and Revenues," pp. 246; also John T. *Gurash Committee Report*, pp. xvii and 14.

45. Bartell, "Costs and Revenues," p. 256.

46. Ibid.

47. An example of this was reported in "Missouri Parents Set Up Own School to Counter an Anti-Christian Philosophy," *New York Times*, October 2, 1972, p. 28. See also " Statement of the American Association of Christian Schools," (Testimony before the House Committee on Ways and Means, U.S. Congress, August 1972; processed).

48. U.S. Bureau of the Census, *Current Population Reports*, Series P-25, no. 448, "Population Estimates and Projections," (August 6, 1970), Table 2, p. 28.

49. Brown, "Enrollment in Nonpublic Schools," pp. 193, 195, 208.

50. Bartell, "Costs and Revenues," p. 256.

51. Ibid.

Chapter 3
The Economics of a Mixed Supply

1. Vivian T. Thayer, *Formative Ideas in American Education from the Colonial Period to the Present* (New York: Dodd, Mead and Company, 1965), p. 116.

2. Charles Beard and Mary Beard, *The Rise of American Civilization* (New York: MacMillan Company, 1927), p. 760.

3. Ibid., p. 810. A different interpretation of labor's involvement is offered by Samuel S. Bowles, "Unequal Education and the Reproduction of the Social Division of Labor," *Review of Radical Political Economics* 3 (Fall/Winter 1971): 7.

4. See Beard and Beard, *American Civilization*, p. 811; also Thayer, *American Education*, p. 117, lists a number of federal revenue acts between 1785 and 1862 which included subsidies for education, all in the form of grants to the states. Originally, public schools were established to "fill the gap" left by the private schools; but, as public goods theory would predict, they soon became the dominant form in many areas. See "Historical Aspects of the Debate on Education," in A.C.F. Beales, *Education: A Framework for Choice; Papers on Historical Economic, and Administrative Aspects of Choice in Education and Its Finance*, 2nd ed. (London: Institute of Economic Affairs, 1970), pp. 4-5.

5. See Chapter 1, pp. 5-6. For a discussion of the ideas of these economists see E.G. West, *Education and the State: A Study in Political Economy* (London: Institute of Economic Affairs, 1965), Ch. 3.

6. Adam Smith, *An Inquiry into the Nature and Causes of the Wealth of Nations* (Homewood, Illinois: Richard D. Irwin, 1963), Book 5, pp. 284-86.

7. Ibid., pp. 268-69.

8. Ibid., pp. 269-70. Smith believed that if teachers were salaried, they would become lazy and the quality of instruction would decline.

9. West, *Education and the State*, pp. 122-24.

10. John Stuart Mill, "On Liberty," in George R. La Noue, *Educational Vouchers: Concepts and Controversies* (New York: Teachers College Press, 1972), p. 4.

11. The distinction between a *service* and a *commodity* is discussed in detail in Victor Fuchs, *The Service Economy* (New York: National Bureau of Economic Research, 1968), pp. 14-15.

12. This difficulty is discussed in Alice M. Rivlin, "Measuring Perfor-

mance in Education," a paper prepared for the Conference on Research in Income and Wealth, National Bureau of Economic Research (Washington: processed, 1972).

13. This point is made by Fuchs, *Service Economy*, p. 194.

14. A number of studies have tried to determine whether there are economies of scale in the production of schooling. John Riew, in a 1966 article, "Economies of Scale in High School Operation," *Review of Economics and Statistics* (August 1966), pp. 280-87, found significant economies of scale. The equation which he estimated, however, was very poorly specified. Most other investigators have found no economies or diseconomies, the best of these studies being Werner Z. Hirsch, *The Economics of State and Local Government* (New York: McGraw-Hill, 1970), pp. 176-82 and Table 8-1. This latter result is consistent with the findings of the study by Averch et al., cited in Chapter 1, that we appear to be in a "flat region" with regard to education technology. Note that implicit in all of these analyses is the assumption that education must take place in schools.

For purposes of discussing the theory of optimal provision of schooling, it is convenient to assume that all outputs are produced jointly. If some of these outputs are in fact produced separately, then we may simply treat a school as two or more independent schools—see next section.

15. See Martin O'Donoghue, *Economic Dimensions in Education* (Chicago: Aldine Publishers, 1971), pp. 44-46, 73, and 83-84. For example, is learning to appreciate classical music classed as investment or as durable consumption—or no benefit at all, but merely a change in tastes?

16. The most often cited work on this subject is Burton A. Weisbrod, *External Benefits of Public Education: An Economic Analysis* (Princeton: Industrial Relations Section, Princeton University, 1964). Most writers agree that education is a mixed good. However, for simplicity they frequently treat it as purely public or private. See, for example, the recent "Symposium on Efficiency Aspects of Local School Finance," *Journal of Political Economy* 81 (January/February 1973):158-202. Note that to the extent that education is merely a screening device, the social benefits must be of a noneconomic kind.

17. See, for example, West, *Education and the State* Chapters 3-7, and Milton Friedman, "The Role of Government in Education," in *Capitalism and Freedom* (Chicago: University of Chicago Press, 1962).

18. See Richard Musgrave, *Theory of Public Finance* (New York: McGraw-Hill, 1959), pp. 134-42. Put more formally, the first-order condition for "optimal provision" of a mixed good is the following:

$$V_a^1 + \sum_{i=1}^{s} V_b^i = V_a^2 + \sum_{i=1}^{s} V_b^i = \ldots = V_a^s \sum_{i=1}^{s} V_b^i = C_q$$

where V_R is read as the marginal value to the ith person from his or her consuming an additional unit of output R, a and b are the private and public outputs respectively, and C_q is the marginal cost of good q. (See E.J. Mishan, "The Relationship between Joint Products, Collective Goods, and External Effects," *Journal of Political Economy* 77 (May/June 1969): 329-48.

19. For a discussion of the impact this demand has on optimality conditions, see James Duesenberry, *Income, Saving, and the Theory of Consumer Behavior* (Cambridge: Harvard University Press, 1949), pp. 93-110.

20. This problem in general is discussed in Gordon Tullock, *Private Wants, Public Means: An Economic Analysis of the Desirable Scope of Government* (New York: Basic Books, 1970), pp. 105-108. He points out that the increased standardization of products as a result of having the government, rather than the private market, provide them is merely a change in degree, not a change in kind.

21. This distinction is elaborated by Albert Rees, "Information Networks in Labor Markets," *American Economic Review* 56 (May 1966):559-66.

22. A major problem with the market and consumer sovereignty is that it may be very costly for families to switch schools—i.e., "searching" over an unconstrained range of alternatives may be very expensive. One solution proposed for the case of day care is to have institutions of established quality—see Richard R. Nelson and Michael Krashinsky, "Public Control and the Economic Organization of Day Care for Young Children," (New Haven, unpublished, 1973).

It was principally because he thought parents would not be able to make good choices that John Stuart Mill believed the state should intervene in education (see West, *Education and the State*, pp. 123-24). It might be noted that much of this difficulty may lie in parents having no experience in selecting schools. If so, the market would presumably improve as an allocation mechanism as time went on.

23. Recently some have argued persuasively that no preferences are exogenous to the economic system and that in fact schooling plays a key role in helping to form future preferences. See Herbert Gintis, "Toward a Political Economy of Education: A Radical Critique of Ivan Illich's *Deschooling Society*," *Harvard Educational Review* 42 (February 1972):70-96.

24. See Tullock, *Private Wants*, p. 31.

25. This point is strongly made by John Brandl, "Public Service Outputs of Higher Education: An Exploratory Essay," in *Outputs of Higher Education: Their Identification, Measurement, and Evaluation*, Seminar

held in Washington, D.C. May 3-5, 1970, conducted by the Western Interstate Commission for Higher Education, Boulder, Colorado, pp. 85-91. He argues that "academic organization is, then, the institutionalized antithesis of the firm or government bureau" (p. 87).

26. See note 14. While the evidence suggests that over a very wide range schooling is a constant-cost operation, there may be a minimum efficient size. And, as Milton Friedman has pointed out (*Capitalism and Freedom*, p. 93), in rural areas with low population, a natural monopoly situation may exist.

27. See Musgrave, *Public Finance*, pp. 13-14. The debate over whether such wants exist is in part a philosophical one. A slightly different interpretation is to see this type of demand as the controlling group in society wishing to supplement individuals' preferences regarding the amount consumed. In both cases there is a paternalistic overtone to "merit" goods —note that the goods or services in question are ones which appear to generate largely private benefits. It should also be noted that the existence of merit wants implies direct interference with consumer sovereignty.

28. See West, *Education and the State*, Chapter 1.

29. See Richard Musgrave, above. Yoram Barzel has also demonstrated the tradeoff between greater standardization of product and higher cost of it—see Yoram Barzel, "Two Propositions on the Optimum Level of Producing Collective Goods," *Public Choice* 6 (Spring 1969): 31-38.

30. See Marc Blaug, "Economic Aspects of Vouchers for Education," in A.C.F. Beales, *Education*, pp. 23-47. Blaug notes that in part the issue of constraining choice is in part a philosophical debate over the role of the state and the unit of welfare (i.e., parents or children) in a school subsidy program.

31. As Musgrave points out, the nature of the good may be such that public production is the most efficient way to capture these benefits. See Musgrave, *Public Finance*, pp. 46-47.

32. Note that this model assumes the various outputs of schooling are produced jointly. Also, it should be noted that this analysis is in the spirit of James M. Buchanan, *The Demand and Supply of Public Goods* (Chicago: Rand McNally, 1968).

33. This subsidy scheme is developed in detail diagramatically in Richard Musgrave, "Provision for Social Goods," in Margolis and Guitton, *Public Expenditures*, pp. 135-42.

34. This analysis assumes that true private preferences are known. As Mark Pauly points out, there are incentives for individuals to hide their preferences, to induce society to increase its subsidy, rather than society taking a "free ride." Clearly it makes a difference in the case of joint production, whether the public or the private benefits are added at margin;

Pauly presents a scheme for subsidy where bargaining between an individual and society is allowed. See Mark V. Pauly, "Mixed Public and Private Financing of Education: Efficiency and Feasibility," *American Economic Review* 57 (December 1967): 120-30.

35. For a discussion of how the present system works, see Noel M. Edelson, and Timothy Hogan and Robert Shelton, both in *Journal of Political Economy*, "Symposium."

36. As James Duesenberry has shown, in this case a progressive tax subsidy scheme (here viewed as the property tax plus a tax in the form of a limit on the amount wealthier people may consume) may be an efficient means to provide the good. See James Duesenberry, *Income and Saving*, pp. 100-102.

37. A similar diagram for a particular case may be found in Barzel, "Private Schools and Public School Finance," in the *Journal of Political Economy*, "Symposium," p. 182. He fails to distinguish, however, between cost of schooling and cost to the parent.

38. This is the approach used by Robin Barlow, "Efficiency Aspects of Local School Finance," *Journal of Political Economy* 78 (September/October 1970), pp. 1028-40; and by all authors in the *Journal of Political Economy*, "Symposium."

39. Even the simplest voucher, reimbursement for the share of marginal cost represented by public benefits, may be unwarranted if attendance at the private school generates social disbenefits. For a discussion of "vouchers" in this context and why a discontinuity in prices may be desirable, see James Tobin, "On Limiting the Domain in Inequality," *The Journal of Law and Economics* 13 (October 1970): 271-73.

40. See National Conference of Catholic Bishops, "To Teach as Jesus Did," a Pastoral Message on Education, printed in *Origins: N.C. Documentary Service* 2 (November 23, 1972): 360.

41. This analysis has assumed that the local school district and the market area are coterminus. In fact, people may be free to move about several local school districts in the same geographic area. In this case, other public school systems may provide many of the benefits ascribed here to the private school. Movement may also serve to make population more homogeneous, and hence the equal-consumption constraint may imply less reduction of total benefits than otherwise. For a discussion of how the existence of many districts may affect optimality, see Charles M. Tiebout, "A Pure Theory of Local Expenditures," *Journal of Political Economy* 64 (October 1956): 416-24.

42. This is rigorously demonstrated in David S. Mundel, "Federal Aid to Higher Education and the Poor" (Cambridge, unpublished manuscript, 1971), pp. 96-97.

43. See Marc Blaug, "Vouchers for Education," p. 32.

Chapter 4
Nonpublic Schools and the Public Sector

1. *NAIS Report,* nos. 35 (December 1970), 39 (January 1972), and 43 (January 1973). For a discussion of defects in other nonpublic schools, see *Tax Credits for Nonpublic Education; Hearings before the Committee on Ways and Means, House of Representatives,* 92nd Cong., 2nd sess. (Washington: Committee, 1973), pp. 90-98.

2. Richard M. Nixon, "Remarks of the President to Sixty-Ninth Annual Convention, National Catholic Educational Association" (speech delivered at Philadelphia, April 6, 1972; processed), p. 5.

3. This approach is essentially the same one used by Thomas Swartz, in doing a similar study for the President's Commission on School Finance. See Thomas R. Swartz, "The Estimated Marginal Cost of Absorbing All Nonpublic Students into the Public School System," in Frank J. Fahey, director, *Economic Problems of Nonpublic Schools* (A Report submitted to the President's Commission on School Finance by the University of Notre Dame, Office of Education Research, 1971), pp. 301-350. Swartz's study is for an earlier year and uses slightly different assumptions about capacity and costs.

4. There would be some increase in books and other supplies, but these are a very small part of the cost of instruction. It is also assumed here that costs imposed on other students would be negligible—i.e., that the schools have facilities to handle more students and, as a number of recent studies have shown, small changes in class sizes do not represent a decline in the amount of education received (see, for example, James W. Guthrie et al., *Schools and Inequality* (Cambridge: MIT Press, 1971).)

5. Swartz, "Marginal Cost of Absorbing," pp. 597-98. The data he used were not available for more recent years.

6. This assumes that the bonds are issued as serial bonds, maturing in one to twenty-five years (i.e., 1/25th of the bonds are retired each year), and having an interest rate of 5.5 percent. These parameters are typical of recent school bond issues—see U.S. Office of Education, *Bond Sales for Public School Purposes,* 1970-71 (Washington: U.S. Government Printing Office, 1972).

7. John T. Gurash, chairman, *The Report of the Archdiocesan Advisory Committee on the Financial Crisis of Catholic Schools in Philadelphia and Surrounding Counties* (Philadelphia: Committee, 1972), Table 5-9, p. 119—hereafter referred to as the *Gurash Committee Report.*

8. Ibid., Table 5-7, p. 117.

9. For example, in Philadelphia, the Gurash Committee estimates that while in the first year the state would pick up none of the burden, by the third year of transfers the state would be contributing over three-quarters of the increased cost. Ibid., p.119.

10. See Wilbur J. Cohen, director, *The Financial Implications of Changing Patterns of Nonpublic School Operations in Chicago, Detroit, Milwaukee and Philadelphia,* A Report Submitted to the President's Commission on School Finance by the School of Education, University of Michigan (Washington: Commission, 1972), pp. 92, 100. Note that this evidence is consistent with the "social" argument made in support of aid—see below.

11. Catholic schools alone had an operating deficit of at least $965 million. (Interpolated from data presented in Ernest J. Bartell, "Costs and Revenues of Nonpublic Elementary and Secondary Education: The Past, Present, and Future of Roman Catholic Schools," in Frank J. Fahey, *Nonpublic Schools,* p. 256.)

12. New York Department of City Planning, "Three Out of Ten: The Nonpublic Schools of New York City" (Department of City Planning, City of New York, March 1972; processed), p. 75.

13. Catholic family data from Dennis J. Dugan, "The Determinants of Enrollment in Catholic Schools," in Fahey, *Nonpublic Schools,* pp. 428, 433, 438; data on all families from U.S. Bureau of the Census, *Census of Population, 1970, General Social and Economic Characteristics,* Final Report PC(1)-C-27, *Missouri* (1972), Tables 89, 124, 135.

14. U.S. Bureau of the Census, *Current Population Reports,* Series P-60, no. 90, "Money Income in 1972 of Families and Persons in the United States" (Washington: U.S. Government Printing Office, 1973), Table 3, p. 24.

15. Nixon, "Remarks," p. 5.

16. Ibid.

17. Cohen, *Financial Implications,* pp. 24-30. It should be noted here that this evidence, and this argument, run counter to the suggestion that the burden of the nonpublic schools closing would be borne by the central cities.

18. National Catholic Educational Association, *A Report on U.S. Catholic Schools, 1970-71* (Washington: NCEA Research Department, 1971), p. 27. It should be noted here that many of the blacks enrolled are non-Catholic, occupying seats left vacant by deported Catholics. If public subsidies made these schools sufficiently attractive to bring Catholics back, the minority students would be forced out.

19. Richard Nixon, "Remarks," p. 8.

20. *Report of the New York State Commission on the Quality, Cost and Financing of Elementary and Secondary Education* (New York: Commission, 1972), vol. 1, p. 5.21—hereafter referred to as the *Fleischman Commission Report.*

21. See Matthew B. Miles, ed., *Innovation in Education* (New York: Columbia Teachers College, 1964), esp. Chs. 1 and 25 written by Miles. At the conclusion of Chapter 1, he has an extensive bibliography relating to educational innovation.

22. Richard R. Nelson, "Issues and Suggestions for the Study of Industrial Organization in a Regime of Rapid Technical Change," in Victor R. Fuchs, ed., *Policy Issues and Research Opportunities in Industrial Organization,* Fiftieth Anniversary Colloquium III (New York: National Bureau of Economic Research, 1972), pp. 47-50.

23. Ibid., pp. 15-18. Note that these categories are very similar to the threefold typology of education policies discussed in Chapter 1: spend more money, reallocate resources, or reorganize resources.

24. Much has been written on this subject in recent years. See, for example, Charles E. Silberman, *Crisis in the Classroom: The Re-making of American Education* (New York: Random House, 1970), esp. Ch. 5, "The Failures of Educational Reform"; also Anthony G. Oettinger, *Run, Computer, Run: The Mythology of Innovation in Education* (Cambridge: Harvard University Press, 1969). Oettinger points out that frequently developers of innovations divert resources from their development to premature promotion and diffusion efforts (see p. 7). A principal reason why these tactics are successful is the resistance of schools to evaluation—on this, see Richard Colvard, "The Colleges and the 'Arkansas Purchase' Controversy," and Allen H. Barton and David E. Wilder, "Research and Practice in the Teaching of Reading: A Progress Report," Chs. 5 and 16 in Miles, *Innovation in Education,* pp. 117-56 and 361-98, respectively.

25. As Nelson has pointed out, in recent years the schools have failed to respond to such changes in demand as how to teach the urban poor with non-middle-class values, what to do with bored middle-class youngsters, and how to operate integrated schools (Nelson, "Issues and Suggestions," p. 48).

26. See Daniel E. Griffiths, "Administrative Theory and Change in Organizations," Ch. 18, in Miles, *Innovation in Education,* pp. 425-36.

27. See Gerhard Eichholtz and Everett M. Rogers, "Resistance to the Adoption of Audio-Visual Aids by Elementary School Teachers: Contrasts and Similarities to Agricultural Innovation," and Sloan R. Wayland, "Structural Features of American Education as Basic Factors in Innova-

124

tion," Chs. 12 and 23 in Miles, *Innovation in Education*, pp. 299-316 and 587-614, respectively.

28. See Daniel E. Griffiths, "Administrative Theory," and Matthew B. Miles, "On Temporary Systems," Ch. 19 in Miles, *Innovation in Education*.

29. This may be in part offset by the fact that when neither you nor your competitors can expand your respective market shares, there is no reason for you not to fully disseminate any innovation. However, there is also little incentive to set up an effective diffusion apparatus (on both points, see Nelson, "Issues and Suggestions," pp. 51-2).

30. See Eicholtz and Rogers, "Resistance to Adoption." For an excellent treatment of this whole subject, see Everett M. Rogers, *Diffusion of Innovations* (New York: Free Press of Glencoe, 1962).

31. That is, real innovation will only be achieved through a mutation-selection process—see Nelson, "Issues and Suggestions," pp. 49-50, 57.

32. See Wayland, "American Education," pp. 598-602.

33. See U.S. Office of Education, *Experimental Schools Program: 1971 Experimental School Projects; Three Education Plans*, DHEW (OE) 72-42 (1972); also *The Fleischman Commission Report*, p. 5.21.

34. See Rogers, *Diffusion of Innovations*, pp. 311-14; also Robert S. Fox and Ronald Lippitt, "The Innovation of Classroom Mental Health Practices," in Miles, *Innovation in Education*, pp. 271-98.

35. Wayland, "American Education," p. 598.

36. Some authors have argued that links between the innovator and the target system are *the* essential difficulty—see C.P. Loomis, "Social Change and Social Systems," in E.A. Tisyakian, ed., *Sociological Theory, Values, and Sociocultural Change* (New York: Free Press of Glencoe, 1963), pp. 185 ff; also Henry M. Brickell, "State Organization for Educational Change: A Case Study and A Proposal," in Miles, *Innovation in Education*, pp. 493-532. That links between public and nonpublic schools are weak was one finding of the Fleischman Commission study of New York State. It concluded that "there are no effective links between the public and nonpublic sectors to allow for the dissemination of information on innovative techniques." *(Fleischman Commission Report*, p. 5.21.)

37. In fact, racial segregation in northern public schools has been worsening over the last three years. See U.S. Department of Health, Education, and Welfare, "HEW News," January 13, 1972.

38. *Brown* v. *Board of Education*, 347 U.S. 483 (1954), p. 7.

39. See Louis R. Gary et al., "The Collapse of Nonpublic Education: Rumor or Reality?" The Report on Nonpublic Education in the State of New York for the New York State Commission on the Quality, Cost and

Financing of Elementary and Secondary Education (New York: Commission, 1971; processed), vol. 1, Ch. 5 and vol. 2, "Special Views."

Appendix 4A
The Constitutional Issues in Aid to Nonpublic Schools

1. Many state constitutions, in fact, contain more explicitly restrictive clauses. The most well known of these, and a model for many others, is the so-called Blaine Amendment to the New York State constitution:

Neither the state nor any subdivision thereof shall use its property or credit or any public money, or authorize or permit either to be used, directly or indirectly, in aid or maintenance, other than for examination or inspection, of any school or institution of learning wholly or in part under the control or direction of any religious denomination, or in which any denominational tenent or doctrine is taught, but the legislature may provide for the transportation of children to and from any school or institution of learning. [Article XI, Section 3]

2. Actually, the Court dealt indirectly with this issue as far back as 1899, when it ruled that public aid to church-controlled hospitals was permissible since the hospital was not a part of the church's religious activities per se *(Bradfield* v. *Roberts,* 175 U.S. 291 (1899). For a good summary of this legal history, see Charles M. Whelan and Paul A. Freund, *Legal and Constitutional Problems of Public Support for Nonpublic Schools,* submitted to the President's Commission on School Finance (Washington: Commission, 1971).

3. *Everson* v. *Board of Education,* 330 U.S. 1 (1947).

4. The Court viewed this aid as akin to providing police or fire protection, which is extended to all citizens, regardless of religious affiliation. In part the issue here was what Whelan calls the "indissoluble tension between the twin constitutional policies of No Establishment and Free Exercise of religion" (Whelan, *Legal and Constitutional Problems,* p. 18).

5. *Abington School District* v. *Schempp,* 374 U.S. 203 (1963).

6. Ibid., at 305.

7. *Board of Education* v. *Allen,* 392 U.S. 236 (1968).

8. *Walz* v. *Tax Commission,* 397 U.S. 664 (1970). This decision also stressed the fact that such tax relief had been given to churches for nearly 200 years.

9. *Lemon* v. *Kurtzman,* 403 U.S. 602 (1971), together with *Early* v. *Di Censo* and *Robinson* v. *Di Censo,* nos. 569 and 570 (1970).

10. Ibid., at 614. The Court also asserted that it was permissible "to provide church-related schools with secular, neutral, or nonideological services, facilities, or materials." (Ibid., at 616.)

11. Ibid., at 612, 613.

12. *Committee for Public Education and Religious Liberty* v. *Nyquist,* no. 72-694 (slip opinion); *Levitt* v. *Committee for Public Education and Religious Liberty,* no. 72-269 (slip opinion); and *Sloan* v. *Lemon,* no. 72-459 (slip opinion)—all decided June 25, 1973.

13. *Committee for Public Education and Religious Liberty* v. *Nyquist,* at 17.

14. For a discussion of the last three distinctions, see Charles M. Whelan, *Legal and Constitutional Problems,* pp. 55 ff.

15. The recent Court decisions seemed particularly concerned with this distinction—*Committee for Public Education and Religious Liberty* v. *Nyquist,* at 16-18.

16. For a discussion of the most recent legal developments, see *Church and State* 27 (March 1974): 3, 11-13; and *Church and State* 27 (July/August 1974): 1, 6-8.

17. President's Panel on Nonpublic Education, *Nonpublic Education and the Public Good* (Washington: U.S. Government Printing Office, 1972), pp. 28-30.

Chapter 5
Public Policy for Existing Nonpublic Schools

1. *Public Aid to Nonpublic Education,* a staff report of the President's Commission on School Finance (Washington: Commission, 1971).

2. See *New York Times,* October 10, 1972.

3. For a complete description of these various "in-kind" aid programs, see "Local Cooperative Programs between the Public and Nonpublic Schools," in Donald A. Erickson and George F. Madaus, *Issues of Aid to Nonpublic Schools,* vol. 3; *Public Assistance Programs for Nonpublic Schools,* submitted to the President's Commission on School Finance (Washington: Commission, 1972), Ch. 4.

4. These indirect subsidies might also be viewed as in part offsetting the "double burden" that parents of nonpublic school children must allegedly bear. Recently, the general public seems to have become aware of the subsidy nature of these exemptions: a 1971 survey found that over half the people in nine of the ten cities surveyed were in favor of eliminating the tax-exempt status of nonpublic schools (see "City Taxes and Services: Citizens Speak Out," *Nation's Cities* (August 1971): 9.)

5. Calculation was made by assuming an average value of land and buildings of $250,000 for Catholic elementary schools, $600,000 for Catholic diocesan secondary schools, $800,000 for Catholic private secon-

dary schools, $500,000 for other sectarian schools, and $1,315,000 for nonsectarian schools; these values are consistent with data in *The Handbook of Private Schools* (Boston: Porter Sargent, 1971). A tax rate of 2.5 percent was used, approximately the average in the urban Northeast—this rate is one-half that which is estimated to apply to all church property in Joseph A. Ruskay, and Richard A. Osserman, *Half Way to Tax Reform* (Bloomington: Indiana University Press, 1970), pp. 14-15. The total estimated value of sectarian schools is $8.3 billion, or about 15 percent of the total value of church property according to Ruskay and Osserman.

6. This assumes parents of students were at least representative of donors to the various schools and churches, which seem reasonable since, as noted earlier (see Chapter 2), there is reason to believe that much or most of the church subsidies are paid for by parents with children enrolled in the schools. Church subsidies to schools were assumed to come from deductible contributions. On the basis of past Internal Revenue Service data (see U.S. Internal Revenue Service, *Statistics of Income–1970 Individual Income Tax Returns,* no. 79 (10-72), 1972) and existing tax rates, it was assumed that 75 percent of these donations were reported and that the average applicable tax rate was 22 percent. It was assumed that all "gift" income was itemized and that the average applicable rate was 33 percent.

7. See National Catholic Educational Association, *U.S. Catholic Schools,* 1972-73 (Washington: NCEA Research Department, 1973), p. 33.

8. See Sidney P. Marland, Jr., "Public Policy and the Private Schools" (speech delivered to the National Catholic Educational Association, Philadelphia, April 3, 1972; processed), p. 6.

9. See *NAIS Report,* no. 49 (February 1974), p. 10; and "School Statistics of the Lutheran Church-Missouri Synod: September 1973," Table 26.

10. The general legal opinion is that the constitution would probably require public schools to accept "part-time" students. See *Report of the New York State Commission on the Quality, Cost and Financing of Elementary and Secondary Education,* vol. 1 (New York: Commission, 1972), p. 5A-4.

11. Frequently where dual enrollment is implemented, enrollments decline more rapidly. See John T. Gurash, chairman, *The Report of the Archdiocesan Advisory Committee on the Financial Crisis of Catholic Schools in Philadelphia and Surrounding Counties* (Philadelphia: Committee, 1972); also Donald A. Erickson et al., "Crisis in Illinois Nonpublic Schools," Final Research Report to the Elementary and Secondary Nonpublic Schools Study Commission, State of Illinois (Commission, 1971; processed), pp. 2-5, 2-6.

12. Ernest J. Bartell, "Costs and Revenues of Nonpublic Elementary

and Secondary Education: The Past, Present, and Future of Roman Catholic Schools," in Frank J. Fahey, *Economic Problems of Nonpublic Schools,* Submitted to the President's Commission on School Finance by the Office of Educational Research, University of Notre Dame (Washington: Commission, 1972), p. 256.

13. In part this is the result of statements by high church officials seeking support for the schools from which many Catholics inferred that any closing of schools, even for purposes of consolidation, represents a defeat and a first step toward total collapse of the system—see Louis R. Gary and K.C.Cole, "The Politics of Aid—and a Proposal for Reform," *Saturday Review* 55 (July 22, 1972): 31-33.

14. See Louis R. Gary and Associates, "The Collapse of Nonpublic Education: Rumor or Reality?" The Report on Nonpublic Education in the State of New York for the New York State Commission on the Quality, Cost and Financing of Elementary and Secondary Education (New York: Commission, 1971), vol. 1, p. 4-12.

15. See Bartell, "Costs and Revenues," p. 249; also *Gurash Committee Report,* p. xvii. In part this is the result of the fact that as families' incomes rise, their marginal propensity to contribute to the chruch declines—see Gary and Associates, "Collapse of Nonpublic Education," vol. 1, pp. 2-13, 2-14.

16. *Gurash Committee Report*, p. 29.

17. See *Tilton* v. *Richardson,* 403 U.S. 672 (1971). Secular colleges and universities avoid this difficulty by obtaining aid for dormitories, laboratories and other nonclassroom buildings. Even if such grants were found legal, moreover, it is not likely they would have much of an impact since Catholic schools are closing most rapidly in the suburbs, where schools are the fewest and where it is envisioned construction would take place.

18. The basic argument is that while an expenditure program represents active government involvement with sectarian schools, tax credits or deductions actually amount to redefinitions of "income" in the Internal Revenue Code. See Boris I. Bittker, "Churches, Taxes and the Constitution," *Yale Law Journal* 78 (July 1969): 1285-1310. Hawaii, Minnesota and California, in fact, have laws providing for tax credits. The Minnesota and California laws, however, are currently being challenged in federal court.

19. See President's Panel on Nonpublic Education, *Nonpublic Education and the Public Good* (Washington: U.S. Government Printing Office, 1972), pp. 32-33.

20. Ibid., p. 36. The panel estimates the costs of aid to the poor at $30 million in 1972-73, less than these people are receiving under Title I.

21. Ibid., p. 38.

22. For a comprehensive discussion of the various alternatives, see Center for the Study of Public Policy, "Education Vouchers: A Preliminary Report on Financing Education by Payments to Parents," (Cambridge, Massachusetts: Center, 1970). Note that the case for vouchers must rest on a view of schooling as a heterogeneous good, and consumers with heterogeneous tastes.

23. U.S. Congress, House, H.R. 17072, "A Bill to Amend the Internal Revenue Code of 1954 to Allow a Credit against the Individual Income Tax for Tuition Paid for Elementary or Secondary Education of Dependents," 92nd Cong., 2nd sess. (1972), sec. 1.

24. See press release, "Statement by the Honorable George P. Shultz, Secretary of the Treasury, before the House Ways and Means Committee," August 14, 1972.

25. Justice Byron R. White, in his dissent in *Lemon* v. *Kurtzman,* makes an interesting point which he describes as the "insoluble paradox": "The State cannot finance secular instruction if it permits religion to be taught in the same classroom; but if it exacts a promise that religion not be so taught—a promise the school and its teachers are quite willing and on this record able to give—and enforces it, it is then entangled in the 'no entanglement' aspect of the Court's Establishment Clause jurisprudence." *Lemon* v. *Kurtzman,* at 688.

26. As Chapter 2 pointed out, many church-related schools now take advantage of these provisions by having special collections and "suggested" parental contributions in lieu of higher tuitions. See Erickson et al., "Crisis," pp. 4-31, 4-32.

27. In 1970, the percentage of taxpayers in various income classes who itemized deductions were as follows:

Under $5,000:	19%	$10,000-15,000:	75%
$5,000-10,000:	52%	Over $15,000:	91%

(Source: Internal Revenue Service, *Statistics of Income,* p. 103.)

28. Bartell, "Costs and Revenues," p. 256.

29. For a discussion of diversity in the public sector, see Anthony Downs, "Competition and Community Schools," in Henry M. Levin, ed., *Community Control of Schools* (Washington: Brookings Institution, 1970), pp. 219-49.

Bibliography

Books

Abbot, Walter M., S. J., ed. *The Documents of Vatican II*. New York: America Press, 1966.

Bartell, Ernest et al. *Catholic Education in St. Louis: Allocation and Distribution of Human and Financial Resources*. Notre Dame: Office for Educational Research, University of Notre Dame Press, 1968.

Baumol, William J. *Welfare Economics and the Theory of the State*. Cambridge: Harvard University Press, 1965.

Beales, A.C.F. *Education: A Framework for Choice; Papers on Historical, Economic, and Administrative Aspects of Choice in Education and Its Finance*. 2nd ed. London: Institute of Economic Affairs, 1970.

Beard, Charles and Beard, Mary. *The Rise of American Civilization*. New York: MacMillan Company, 1927.

Becker, Gary S. *Human Capital: A Theoretical and Empirical Analysis with Special Reference to Education*. New York: National Bureau of Economic Research, 1964.

Berg, Ivar. *The Great Training Robbery*. New York: Praeger Publishers, 1970.

Brown, Kenneth M. *Catholic Education in Atlanta: An Economic Analysis*. Notre Dame: Office for Educational Research, University of Notre Dame, 1971.

Buchanan, James M. *The Demand and Supply of Public Goods*. Chicago: Rand McNally, 1968.

Burkehead, Jesse. *Input and Output in a Large City High School*. Syracuse: Syracuse University Press, 1967.

Center for the Study of Public Policy. *Education Vouchers: A Preliminary Report on Financing Education by Payments to Parents*. Cambridge: Center, 1970.

Coons, John E. et al. *Private Wealth and Public Education*. Cambridge: Bellnap Press of Harvard University Press, 1970.

Cremin, Lawrence, ed. *The Republic and the School: Horace Mann on the Education of Free Men*. Classics in Education no. 1. New York: Teacher's College, Columbia University, 1957.

Dennison, George. *The Lives of Children: The Story of the First Street School*. New York: Random House (Vintage Books), 1969.

Duesenberry, James. *Income, Saving, and the Theory of Consumer Behavior*. Cambridge: Harvard University Press, 1949.

Friedman, Milton. *Capitalism and Freedom*. Chicago: University of Chicago Press, 1962.

Fuchs, Victor. *The Service Economy*. New York: National Bureau of Economic Research, 1968.

Greely, Andrew M. and Rossi, Peter H. *The Education of Catholic Americans*. Garden City: Doubleday, 1966.

Guthrie, James W. et al. *Schools and Inequality*. Cambridge: MIT Press, 1971.

Hansen, W. Lee, ed. *Education, Income and Human Capital*. Conference on Education and Income. New York: National Bureau of Economic Research, 1970.

Hirsch, Werner Z. *The Economics of State and Local Government*. New York: McGraw-Hill, 1970.

Holt, John. *What Do I Do on Monday*. New York: E.P. Dutton & Co., 1970.

Illich, Ivan. *Deschooling Society*. New York: Harper & Row, 1971.

Kraushaar, Otto. *American Nonpublic Schools: Patterns of Diversity*. Baltimore: Johns Hopkins Press, 1972.

Katz, Michael. *The Irony of Early School Reform*. Cambridge: Harvard University Press, 1968.

Katzman, Martin. *The Political Economy of Urban Schools*. Cambridge: Harvard University Press, 1971.

Kiker, B.F., ed. *Investment in Human Capital*. Columbia, South Carolina: University of South Carolina Press, 1971.

Kozol, Jonathan. *Death at an Early Age: The Destruction of the Hearts and Minds of Negro Children in the Boston Public Schools*. New York: Bantam Books, 1967.

LaNoue, George R. *Educational Vouchers: Concepts and Controversies*. New York: Teachers College Press, 1972.

Levin, Henry M. *Community Control of Schools*. Washington: Brookings Institution, 1969.

McCluskey, Neil G. *Catholic Education Faces Its Future*. Garden City: Doubleday, 1971.

Miles, Matthew B., ed. *Innovation in Education*. New York: Columbia Teachers College, 1964.

Musgrave, Richard. *Theory of Public Finance*. New York: McGraw-Hill, 1959.

National Education Association. *Resolutions and Other Actions*. Detroit, Michigan: NEA Publications, July 1971.

O'Donoghue, Martin. *Economic Dimensions in Education*. Chicago: Aldine Publishers, 1971.

Oettinger, Anthony G. *Run, Computer, Run: The Mythology of Educational Innovation*. Studies in Technology and Society no. 58. Cambridge: Harvard University Press, 1970.

Phillips, Kevin. *The Emerging Republican Majority*. New York: Arlington House, 1969.

Reimer, Everett. *School is Dead: Alternatives in Education*. Garden City: Doubleday, 1971.

Reischauer, Robert D. and Hartman, Robert W., with Sullivan, Daniel J. *Reforming School Finance*. Washington: Brookings Institution, 1973.

Rogers, Everett M. *Diffusion of Innovations*. New York: Free Press of Glencoe, 1962.

Rushay, Joseph A. and Osserman, Richard A. *Half Way to Tax Reform*. Bloomington: Indiana University Press, 1970.

Silberman, Charles. *Crisis in the Classroom: The Remaking of American Education*. New York: Random House, 1970.

Smith, Adam. *An Inquiry into the Nature and Causes of the Wealth of Nations*. Homewood, Illinois: Richard D. Irwin, 1963.

Taeuber, Karl E. and Alma F. *Negroes in Cities: Residential Segregation and Neighborhood Change*. Chicago: Aldine Publishing Company, 1965.

Tax Aid for Parochial and Private Schools: A Compendium of Information for Debaters. Silver Springs, Maryland: Americans United Resource Foundation, August 1972.

Thayer, Vivian T. *Formative Ideas in American Education from the Colonial Period to the Present*. New York: Dodd, Mead and Company, 1965.

Tullock, Gordon. *Private Wants, Public Means: An Economic Analysis of the Desirable Scope of Government*. New York: Basic Books, 1970.

Weisbrod, Burton A. *External Benefits of Public Education: An Economic Analysis*. Princeton: Industrial Relations Section of Princeton University, 1964.

West, E.G. *Education and the State: A Study in Political Economy*. London: Institute of Economic Affairs, 1965.

Wise, Arthur E. *Rich Schools, Poor Schools: The Promise of Equal Educational Opportunity*. Chicago: University of Chicago Press, 1968.

Commission Reports

Averch, Harvey et al. *How Effective is Schooling: A Critical Review and Synthesis of Research Findings*. Final Report to the President's Commission on School Finance. Santa Monica: Rand Corporation, December 1971.

134

Cohen, Wilbur J., director. *The Financial Implications of Changing Patterns of Nonpublic School Operations in Chicago, Detroit, Milwaukee and Philadelphia*. A Report submitted to the President's Commission on School Finance by the School of Education, University of Michigan. Washington: Commission, 1972.

Elford, George, director. *The Catholic Education Study Report*. Indianapolis: Catholic Archdiocese of Indianapolis, 1968.

Erickson, Donald A. and Madaus, George F. *Issues of Aid to Nonpublic Schools, Vol. 3: Public Assistance Programs for Nonpublic Schools*, submitted to the President's Commission on School Finance. Washington: Commission, 1972.

Erickson, Donald A. et al. "Crisis in Illinois Nonpublic Schools," Final Research Report to the Elementary and Secondary Nonpublic Schools Study Commission, State of Illinois. Chicago: Commission, 1971 (processed).

Fahey, Frank J., director. *Economic Problems of Nonpublic Schools*. Submitted to the President's Commission on School Finance by the Office of Educational Research, University of Notre Dame. Washington: Commission, 1972.

Gary, Louis R. et al. *The Collapse of Nonpublic Education: Rumor or Reality?* The Report on Nonpublic Education in the State of New York for the New York State Commission on the Quality, Cost and Financing of Elementary and Secondary Education. 2 vols. New York City: Commission, 1971.

New York Department of City Planning, "Three Out of Ten: The Nonpublic Schools of New York City." New York: Department of City Planning, City of New York, March 1972 (processed).

President's Commission on School Finance, *Schools, People and Money*. Washington: U.S. Government Printing Office, 1972.

President's Panel on Nonpublic Education, *Nonpublic Education and the Public Good*. Washington: U.S. Government Printing Office, 1972.

Public Aid to Nonpublic Education, a study prepared by the staff of the President's Commission on School Finance. Washington: Commission, 1971.

The Report of the Archdiocesan Advisory Committee on the Financial Crisis of Catholic Schools in Philadelphia and Surrounding Counties. Philadelphia: Committee, 1972. By John T. Gurash, Chairman.

Report of the New York State Commission on the Quality, Cost and Financing of Elementary and Secondary Education. Vol. 1. New York: Commission, 1972.

Whelan, Charles M. and Freund, Paul A. *Legal and Constitutional Problems of Public Support for Nonpublic Schools, submitted to the President's Commission on School Finance. Washington: Commission, 1971.*

Articles

Barlow, Robin. "Efficiency Aspects of Local School Finance" *Journal of Political Economy* 78 (September/October 1970): 1028-40.

Barzel, Yoram. "Two Propositions on the Optimum Level of Producing Collective Goods," *Public Choice* 6 (Spring 1969): 31-38.

Benson, Charles S. "Economic Analysis of Institutional Alternatives for Providing Education (Public, Private Sector)," in *Economic Factors Affecting the Financing of Education*, pp. 121-72. Edited by Roe L. John et al. Gainesville: National Education Finance Project, 1970.

Bittker, Boris I. "Churches, Taxes and the Constitution," *Yale Law Journal* 78 (July 1969): 1285-1310.

Bowles, Samuel S. "Schooling and Inequality from Generation to Generation," *Journal of Political Economy* 80 (May/June 1972).

_____. "Towards Equality," *Harvard Educational Review* 38 (Winter 1968): 89-99.

_____. "Unequal Education and the Reproduction of the Social Division of Labor," *The Review of Radical Political Economics* 3 (Fall/Winter 1971): 1-30.

_____. and Gintis, Herbert. "I.Q. in the U.S. Class Structure," *Social Policy* (November/December 1972-January/February 1973): 65-96.

Brandl, John. "Public Service Outputs of Higher Education: An Exploratory Essay," in *Outputs of Higher Education: Their Identification, Measurement and Evaluation*, Seminar held in Washington, D.C., May 3-5, conducted by the Western Interstate Commission for Higher Education, Boulder, Colorado, pp. 85-91.

"City Taxes and Services: Citizens Speak Out," *Nation's Cities* 9 (August 1971): 9.

Coleman, James S. "The Concept of Equality of Educational Opportunity," *Harvard Educational Review* 38 (Winter 1968): 7-22.

Elford, George. "School Crisis—or Parish Crisis?" *Commonweal* 93 (January 29, 1971): 418-420.

Gary, Louis R. and Cole, K. C. "The Politics of Aid and a Proposal for Reform," *Saturday Review of Education* 55 (July 22, 1972): 31-33.

Gintis, Herbert. "Education and the Characteristics of Worker Productivity," *American Economic Review* 61 (May 1971): 266-79.

————. "Toward a Political Economy of Education: A Radical Critique of Ivan Illich's *Deschooling Society*," *Harvard Educational Review* 42 (February 1972): 70-96.

Loomis, C.P. "Social Change and Social Systems," in E.A. Tisyakian, ed., *Sociological Theory, Values, and Sociocultural Change*. New York: Free Press of Glencoe, 1963.

Mishan, E.J. "The Relationship between Joint Products, Collective Goods, and External Effects," *Journal of Political Economy* 77 (May/June 1969): 329-48.

"Missouri Parents Set Up Own School to Counter an Anti-Christian Philosophy," *New York Times* 2 October 1972, p. 28.

Nelson, Richard R. "Issues and Suggestions for the Study of Industrial Organization in a Regime of Rapid Technical Change," in *Policy Issues and Research Opportunities in Industrial Organization*, Fiftieth Anniversary Colloquium III, pp. 40-60. Edited by Victor R. Fuchs. New York: National Bureau of Economic Research, 1972.

Pauly, Mark V. "Mixed Public and Private Financing of Education: Efficiency and Feasibility," *American Economic Review* 57 (December 1967): 120-30.

————. "Optimality, 'Public' Goods, and Local Governments: A General Theoretical Analysis," *Journal of Political Economy* 78 (May/June 1970): 572-85.

Rees, Albert. "Information Networks in Labor Markets," *American Economic Review* 56 (May 1966): 559-66.

Riew, John. "Economies of Scale in High School Operation," *Review of Economics and Statistics* 48 (August 1966): 280-87.

Rist, R.C. "Student Social Class and Teacher Expectations: The Self-Fulfilling Prophecy in Ghetto Education," *Harvard Educational Review* 40 (1970): 411-51.

Rosenthal, Jack. "Study Shows Catholics Having Smaller Families," *New York Times*, 30 May 1972, pp. 1, 5.

Shanahan, Eileen. "2 Parties Push Nonpublic School Aid with Bill for Tax Credits to Parents," *New York Times*, 7 August 1972.

Shultz, T.W. "Investment in Human Capital," *American Economic Review* 51 (February 1961): 1-17.

"Symposium on Efficiency Aspects of Local School Finance," *Journal of Political Economy* 81 (January/February 1973): 158-202.

Thurow, Lester C. "Education and Economic Equality," *Public Interest* 28 (Summer 1972): 66-81.

Tiebout, Charles M. "A Pure Theory of Local Expenditures," *Journal of Political Economy* 64 (October 1956): 416-24.

Tobin, James. "On Limiting the Domain in Inequality," *The Journal of Law and Economics* 13 (October 1970): 271-73.

U.S. Catholic Conference. "To Teach as Jesus Did," U.S. Catholic Bishops' Pastoral Message on Catholic Education, in *Origins* 2 (November 23, 1972).

"Vital Voting Bloc Defects to Nixon," *Washington Post*, 8 October 1972.

Weisbrod, Burton A. "Education and Investment in Human Capital," *Journal of Political Economy* 70 (October 1962): 106-123.

Public Documents

King, Irene A. *Bond Schools for Public School Programs, 1970-71.* Washington: U.S. Office of Education, National Center for Educational Statistics, 1972.

Southeastern Public Education Project, American Friends Service Committee, "Survey of Private Schools Started in Mississippi Since the Passage of the 1964 Civil Rights Act." *Equal Educational Opportunity: Part 3A–Desegregation Under Law,* Hearings before the Senate Select Committee on Equal Educational Opportunity, 91st Cong. 2nd sess. (1970).

"Statement by the Honorable George P. Shultz, Secretary of the Treasury, before the House Ways and Means Committee," U.S. Treasury Department press release, August 14, 1972.

U.S. Bureau of the Census, *Census of Population: 1970 General Social and Economic Characteristics*, Final Report, PC (1)-C (volumes for the respective states). Washington: U.S. Government Printing Office, 1971.

U.S. Bureau of the Census, *Current Population Reports*, Series P-20, No. 222, "School Enrollment: October 1970." Washington: U.S. Government Printing Office, 1971.

U.S. Bureau of the Census, *Current Population Reports*, Series P-20, No. 234, "School Enrollment in the United States: 1971." Washington: U.S. Government Printing Office, 1972.

U.S. Bureau of the Census, *Current Population Reports*, Series P-20, No. 241, "Social and Economic Characteristics of Students: October 1971." Washington: U.S. Government Printing Office, October 1972.

U.S. Bureau of the Census, *Current Population Reports*, Series P-20, No. 260, "Social and Economic Characteristics of Students: October 1972." Washington: U.S. Government Printing Office, February 1974.

138

U.S. Bureau of the Census, *Current Population Reports*, Series P-20, No. 261, "School Enrollment in the United States: October 1973 (Advanced report)." Washington: U.S. Government Printing Office: March 1974.

U.S. Bureau of the Census, *Current Population Reports*, Series P-25, No. 448, "Population Estimates and Projections." Washington: U.S. Government Printing Office, August 1970.

U.S. Bureau of the Census, *Current Population Reports*, Series P-60, No. 90, "Money Income in 1972 of Families and Persons in the United States," Washington: U.S. Government Printing Office, 1973.

U.S. Bureau of the Census, *1970 Census of Population and Housing: Census Tract Reports*, Series PHC (1)—volumes for the respective metropolitan areas. Washington: U.S. Government Printing Office, 1972.

U.S. Bureau of the Census. *Statistical Abstract of the United States 1971*. Washington: U.S. Government Printing Office, 1971.

U.S. Congress. House. H.R. 17072, 92nd Cong., 2nd sess., 1972.

U.S. Congress. House. *Material Relating to Proposals Before the Committee on Ways and Means on the Subject of Aid to Primary and Secondary Education in the Form of Tax Credits and/or Deductions,* 92nd Cong., 2nd sess., 1972.

U.S. Congress. House, Committee on Ways and Means. *Tax Credits for Nonpublic Education: Hearings before the Committee on Ways and Means, House of Representatives*, 92nd Cong., 2nd sess., 1973.

U.S. Congress, Joint Committee on Internal Revenue Taxation. "Staff Study on HR 13495," (processed), February 10, 1972.

U.S. Department of Health, Education and Welfare. *The Effectiveness of Compensatory Education: Summary and Review of the Evidence.* Washington: DHEW, April 1972.

U.S. Department of Health, Education and Welfare, "HEW News," January 13, 1972.

U.S. Department of Health, Education and Welfare," HEW/OCR Press Release," June 18, 1971.

U.S. Department of Health, Education and Welfare, *NCES Bulletin*, No. 12 (June 7, 1972).

U.S. Internal Revenue Service. *Statistics of Income–1970 Individual Income Tax Returns*, No. 79 (10-72). Washington: U.S. Government Printing Office, 1972.

U.S. Office of Education. *Experimental Schools Program: 1971 Experimental School Projects; Three Education Plans*. Washington: DHEW (OE) 72-42, 1972.

U.S. Office of Education. *Nonpublic Schools in Large Cities, 1970-71.* Washington: U.S. Government Printing Office, 1974.

U.S. Office of Education, *Projections of Educational Statistics to 1979-80.* Washington: U.S. Government Printing Office, 1971.

U.S. Office of Education. *Statistics of Nonpublic Elementary and Secondary Schools, 1970-71.* Washington: U.S. Government Printing Office, 1974.

U.S. Office of Education. *Statistics of Public and Nonpublic Elementary and Secondary Day Schools, 1968-69.* Washington: U.S. Government Printing Office, 1971.

U.S., President. "Executive Order No. 11513," March 3, 1970. *Weekly Compilation of Presidential Documents*, Vol. 6 (1970).

U.S. President, "Message to Congress on Elementary and Secondary Education," *Congressional Record*, March 3, 1970.

Unpublished Material

Biemiller, Andrew J. "Statement of Andrew J. Biemiller, Director, Department of Legislation, American Federation of Labor and Congress of Industrial Organization Before the House Committee on Ways and Means on H.R. 16141, the Public and Private Education Assistance Act of 1972." Washington, September 6, 1972 (mimeographed).

Coleman, James S. "Incentives in Education, Existing and Proposed," John Hopkins University, 1970 (mimeographed).

Marland, Sidney P., Jr. "Public Policy and the Private Schools," speech delivered to the National Catholic Education Association, Philadelphia April 3, 1972 (processed).

Mundel, David S. "Federal Aid to Higher Education and the Poor." Cambridge: unpublished manuscript, 1971.

Nelson, Richard R. and Krashinsky, Michael. "Public Control and Economic Organization of Day Care for Young Children." New Haven, 1973 (mimeographed).

Nixon, Richard M. "Remarks of the President to the 69th Annual Convention, National Catholic Education Association," Civic Center, Philadelphia, April 6, 1972 (processed).

Rivlin, Alice M. "Measuring Performance in Education," a paper prepared for the Conference on Research in Income and Wealth, National Bureau of Economic Research. Washington: Brookings Institution, 1972 (processed).

Sachs, Seymour et al. "School State Aid and the System of Finance: Central City, Suburban and Rural Dimensions of Revenue Sharing. Syracuse University, no date (processed).

"Statement of the American Association of Christian Schools," Testimony Before the House Committee on Ways and Means, U.S. Congress, August, 1972 (processed).

Taubman, Paul and Wales, Terence. "Education as an Investment and a Screening Device." New York: National Bureau of Economic Research, 1972 (Mimeographed).

Selected Data Sources

Furno, Orlando F. and Cunco, Paul K. "Cost of Education Index, 1972-73," *School Management* 17 (January 1973).

Gallup Opinion Index, No. 66, December 1970.

Gallup Opinion Index, No. 81, March 1972.

Gallup Opinion Index, No. 87, September 1972.

National Association of Independent Schools. *NAIS Report,* no. 35 (December 1970).

————. *NAIS Report,* no. 39 (January 1972).

————. *NAIS Report,* no. 43 (January 1973).

————. *NAIS Report,* no. 49 (February 1974).

National Catholic Education Association. "NCEA Standard School Survey Form (1972)."

————. *A Report on U.S. Catholic Schools, 1970-71.* Washington: NCEA Research Department, 1971.

————. *A Statistical Report on Catholic Elementary and Secondary Schools for the Years 1967-68 to 1969-70.* Washington: NCEA Research Department, 1970.

————. *U.S. Catholic Schools, 1971-72.* Washington: NCEA Research Department, 1972.

————. *U.S. Catholic Schools, 1972-73.* Washington: NCEA Research Department, 1973.

————. *U.S. Catholic Schools, 1973-74.* Washington: NCEA Research Department, 1974.

National Education Association. *Estimates of School Statistics, 1971-72.* Research Report 1971-R13. Washington: NEA Research Division, 1971.

————. *Estimates of School Statistics, 1972-73,* REA Research Report 1972-R12. Washington & NEA Research Division, 1972.

_____. *Estimates of School Statistics, 1973-74*, Research Report 1973-R8. Washington: NEA Research Division, 1973.

Official Catholic Directory 1970. Boston: P.J. Kennedy & Sons, 1970.

Official Catholic Directory 1971. Boston: P.J. Kennedy & Sons, 1971.

Official Catholic Directory, 1972. Boston: P.J. Kennedy & Sons, 1972.

Senske, Al H. "Lutheran Elementary School Statistics, 1971-72." St. Louis: Board of Parish Education, Lutheran Church, Missouri Synod, 1972 (processed).

_____. "School Statistics of the Lutheran Church—Missouri Synod, September 1973." St. Louis: Board of Parish Education, Lutheran Church—Missouri Synod, 1974 (processed).

Survey of Current Business, August 1972.

"12th Annual Cost of Building Index (1972-73)," *School Management* 17 (June/July 1973): 16-27.

Index

AFL-CIO: in nonpublic schools, 27; opposed to aid, 3
American Federation of Teachers (AFT): opposed to aid, 3
Arkansas: teaching of evolution, 7
Atlanta, 31

Baptist church: opposed to aid, 3
Beard, Charles, 45
Beard, Mary, 45
Benson, Charles S., 10
Birth rate: effect on Catholic schools and public schools, 39
Boarding schools, 23, 37
Bond issues. *See* School bond issues
Brown, Kenneth, 31

California, 3n, 9
Capital expenditures, schools', 64
Carey, Hugh, 8
Catholic church: bishops' statement, 57n; parishes, 29, 36, 96; religious orders, 26, 38; role of schools, 29, 36; Second Vatican Council, 36-37; subsidies to schools, 22, 29, 30n, 38, 54. *See also* Catholic families; Catholic schools
Catholic families: church affiliation, 33, 36, 39; concentration, 17; demand for Catholic school, 33, 35, 37, 69; income, 35, 69; school productivity, effect on, 58; suburbanization, 35, 65. *See also* Catholic schools
Catholic schools: and church subsidies, 22, 29, 38, 54; in city, 19-20, 71; consolidation plan for, 32; contributed services to, 20-22; declining preference for, 26, 33-35, 37; enrollments, 16n, 23, 37; facilities, 22, 35; future of, 39, 104; and income level, 68-69; and innovation, 76; per pupil costs, 26-29; as quasi-public, 22, 29, 54n, 97; relative quality of, 35, 55, 57; revenues, 22, 29; teachers, 26-27; tuition, 29-32. *See also* Catholic church; Catholic families; Finances, nonpublic school; Nonpublic schools
Chicago, 70-71
Child labor laws, 45
Choice, 57; as benefit from nonpublic schooling, 73-74; of nonpublic schooling, 53-54
Cities, 62, 76-77; Catholic schools in, 19-20; nonpublic schools in, 16, 19-20, 62; state aid to, 65; tax base and nonpublic schools, 70, 72, 76-77. *See also* Local government; Suburbs
Class size: in Catholic schools, 22, 26, 35, 38; in public schools, 26
Cohen, Wilbur, 70-71
Coleman Report, 99n
Colorado, 3n
Communal provision, 11; and optimal subsidy, 52-53
Compensatory education, 9-10
Competition: impact on innovation, 74-76
Compulsory school attendance laws, 48-49, 68
Connecticut, 94
Consolidation: of Catholic schools, 32; institutional barriers to, 32n
Contributed services. *See* Catholic schools; Lutheran schools
Costs. *See* Finances, nonpublic school
Crime, 5, 47

Decentralization, 10
Demand, nonpublic school: and consumer sovereignty, 48; data on, 16, 42-43; elasticity of, 31, 42, 44, 58; factors in change of, 35-37; theory of, 16, 41, 47-48. *See also* Catholic schools; Nonpublic schools
Democratic party: and Catholics, 2-3
Dennison, George, 8
Detroit, 70-71
Disadvantaged. *See* Low-income families; Minorities
Discipline, 9
Double burden, 67-68
Dual enrollment, 94, 96
Dugan, Daniel, 36-37

Economists, 52n; paradigm, 11, 46-47; view of education, 5-6, 8, 10
Education: critics of, 7, 47; government involvement in, 11, 45; and intrafamily production, 49; in 19th century, 5, 7, 18n, 45; purpose, 5-7. *See also* Schools
Education production function, 10, 49, 57
Elementary and Secondary Education Act: Title I, 20n, 22, 69, 72, 94-95, 98; Title III, 94
Enrollments: changes in, 22-26; distribution of, 16-20; factors affecting, 17-18, 31,

About the Author

Daniel J. Sullivan, Assistant Professor of Economics at Middlebury College, attended the University of Santa Clara and received the Ph.D. in economics from Yale University in 1974. While at Yale, he served as an advisor to the New Haven, Connecticut, superintendent of schools and as an Intern in Education Evaluation at the U.S. Department of Health, Education, and Welfare. From 1971 to 1973, Professor Sullivan was a research assistant at the Brookings Institution, where he contributed to a number of research projects on the economics of education. He assisted Robert Reischauer and Robert Hartman in writing *Reforming School Finance* (Brookings Institution, 1973) and June O'Neill in writing *Sources of Funds to Colleges and Universities* (Carnegie Commission on Higher Education, 1973).